JOHN GOWER'S POETRY

JOHN GOWER

SELECTED POETRY

EDITED BY
CAROLE WEINBERG

FYFIELD BOOKS
Carcanet   Manchester

First published in 1983 by
CARCANET NEW PRESS LTD.
210 Corn Exchange Buildings   *22/981*
Manchester M4 3BQ

British Library Cataloguing in Publication Data
Gower, John
  Selected poetry.—(Fyfield books)
  I. Title   II. Weinberg, Carole
  821'.1   PR1982

  ISBN 0-85635-415-5

The publisher acknowledges the financial assistance of the
Arts Council of Great Britain

Printed in England by SRP Ltd., Exeter

CONTENTS

INTRODUCTION

IN THE LATE nineteenth century Matthew Arnold, in his *Study of Poetry*, denied Chaucer a place among the first rank of poets because he lacked 'high poetic seriousness'. While he admired Chaucer's style and manner he found him lacking in seriousness of moral purpose. Arnold's emphasis on Chaucer's 'kindly view of human life' seems to have blinded him to the complex moral probing which controlled the texture of Chaucer's narrative. No one, in contrast, has ever accused John Gower, Chaucer's contemporary, of lacking a moral sense. The epithet 'moral' has been attached to him ever since Chaucer, in the well-known verse at the end of Troilus and Criseyde, addressed his poem to 'moral Gower'. Fifteenth and sixteenth century references are respectful of Gower's literary role as a guide to both individual and communal morality, irrespective of the artistic merit of what he wrote. Thomas Berthelette, printer to Henry VIII, published an edition of *Confessio Amantis* in the assurance that readers would find in the work 'arguments and examples of great authority persuading unto virtue'. As for Robert Greene, the late sixteenth-century writer of prose fiction, he repudiated the setting forth of amorous trifles in his *Vision*, published in 1592, and called Gower to witness as an author who placed the seriousness of moral purpose far above mere pleasurability. In Shakespeare's *Pericles* 'ancient Gower' appears on stage to introduce the tale of Pericles which he has already told in the *Confessio Amantis*, and then acts throughout the play as a descriptive and moralizing chorus.

From the sixteenth century onwards critical attention shifted away from Gower's morality and many critics, discerning little artistic merit in the *Confessio*, came to use the term 'moral' as a synonym for tediousness. In recent years, however, a reappraisal of the literary skill of the *Confessio* has to some extent retrieved Gower's reputation among those who study Middle English literature. But the justifiably wide acclaim accorded such gifted contemporaries as Chaucer, Langland, and the Gawain poet has left Gower with a smaller circle of readers than he deserves.

When Chaucer dedicated *Troilus and Criseyde* to his friend it was as the author of the French *Mirour de l'Omme* (The Mirror of Man) and the Latin *Vox Clamantis* (The Voice of One Crying Out) who was being addressed; the *Confessio Amantis* had not yet been written. Both earlier works are moral in theme, admonitory in tone and didactic in purpose. The *Mirour*, over 25,000 lines long and in octosyllabic twelve-line stanzas, opens with an abstract allegory on the origin of sin. It then passes from a general discussion of the seven vices and virtues to specific criticism of the dominance of sin at every level of London society in the 1370's. In *Vox Clamantis* Gower's is the voice crying out against the evils of the age. Gower saw in the irresponsible behaviour of those involved in the Peasants Revolt of 1381 a reflection of the moral anarchy of society, driven to its doom by financial and fleshly lust. In both the *Mirour* and *Vox Clamantis* he placed the blame for worldly ills solely on man himself, and couched the solution in moral terms, the return of all classes of society to virtuous behaviour.

In fourteenth-century political thought the ultimate responsibility for ensuring the right moral ordering of the state lay with the king, and the traditional description of a good king was one who lived virtuously, and abided by the advice of good and wise counsellors (see Ferguson, pp. 70-71). Gower felt strongly on this point, and conscious of his poetic duty, as he saw it, to expose moral irresponsibility, he did not hesitate to publicly criticize his king for unkingly behaviour. His growing disenchantment with Richard II found expression in the revised prologue to the *Confessio Amantis*. The first version of the poem was completed c.1390, the fourteenth year of Richard's reign, and the prologue tells of a meeting on the Thames at which the king asked the poet to write 'som newe thing' for his king to read. The poet, despite 'sekness', agreed to write a poem 'for king Richardes sake' offering 'wisdom to the wise / And pley to hem that lust to pleye'. In the revised prologue of 1392 Gower, omitting any

8

reference to the meeting on the river, claims to have written the poem 'for Engelondes sake'. And in the third recension, dated 1393, the poem is dedicated in a spirit of hope to Henry Lancaster, the future Henry IV. In the same year Henry presented 'esquire John Gower' with an ornamental collar, and five weeks after his coronation in 1399 with an annual grant of two pipes of Gascon wine for life.

But financial need was not a factor in Gower's transfer of allegiance. He came from a landed family with estates in several counties, and was himself involved in the purchase of land, mainly in London and Kent. It is possible that he held some legal or civil office, but he was a man of sufficient means not to have to work for a living. From 1377 he lived in semi-retirement and as a layman in the priory of St. Mary's Overeys in Southwark 'devoting his time mainly to his books and his friends' (Fisher, p. 60). Among his friends he numbered Chaucer, and others with legal, business and court connections. Late in life and having suffered from ill-health for some years he married a fellow parishioner, Agnes Groundolf, probably his nurse. He died in 1408, well into his seventies and blind for several years before his death.

The personal responsibility of a ruler for ensuring the welfare of the realm looms large as a theme in the *Confessio Amantis*. And the prosperity of the realm depends upon the virtuous behaviour of the king. That ruler who

> Attir the lawe of God eshuieth
> The vices, and the vertus suieth,
> His grace shal be suffisant
> To governe al the remenant
> Which longith to his duite;
> So that in his prosperite
> The poeple shal nought ben oppressid.

But insofar as Gower saw an equivalence between the type of behaviour necessary for good kingship and the type of behaviour necessary for good citizenship, the poem focuses on the plight of an individual within society, the unrequited lover Amans. The poem begins with a Prologue, the scene is contemporary England, and Gower, as he had done in the *Mirour* and *Vox Clamantis*, laments the disorderly state of the nation. What Gower sees happening in the Church, for example, reflects what is wrong generally.

> Ther ben also somme, as men seye,
> That folwen Simon ate hieles,
> Whos carte goth upon the whieles
> Of coveitise and worldes pride,
> And Holy Cherche goth beside.

In Book One, however, Gower shifts dextrously from a non-fictional to a fictional mode, and casts himself in the role of the courtly lover Amans. Unable to set the world to rights Gower, instead, will speak of love. The time of the year is May, and Amans is no nearer to achieving success with the lady he loves. 'Bot al of woldes and of wishes / Therof have I my fulle dishes' complains Amans. Dispirited he appeals to Venus, goddess of Love, for help. Venus responds by passing Amans over to her priest, Genius, for cross-examination and instruction. Amans is required to confess his sins against Love while Genius guides him through the catechism. The *Confessio* is divided into eight books each of which, with one exception, is loosely organized round one of the Seven Deadly Sins. The exception is Book Seven, which concerns itself mainly with the nature of kingship. Each of the Seven Deadly Sins is further subdivided into various categories. Thus, in explaining the effect on love of the first Sin, Pride, Genius describes how Pride is bolstered by the behaviour of Hypocrisy, Inobedience, Presumption, Boasting and Vainglory. To make it easier for Amans to see things in perspective, and to give authority to his own statements, Genius draws on a large collection of illustrative tales from many 'olde bokes'. These tales and the confessional framework in which they are set do not, however, transform Amans into a successful lover. Instead he comes to the rueful recognition that he is too advanced in years to be a lover at all. 'For loves luste and lockes hore / In chambre acorden nevermore.'

The device of confession, derived from the medieval penitential manual, imposes an external order on the *Confessio*, but it also affords Genius the opportunity of ranging in encyclopaedic manner over a large number of issues arising from the exploration of the nature of love. For as the narrative progresses it becomes increasingly clear that Genius is not only enlightening Amans as to the irrational nature of his love, but also establishing norms of moral conduct in life as well as in love. Like Amans we, the audience, are being educated both in virtuous loving and in virtuous living.

> For wisdom is at every throwe
> Above all other thing to know
> In Love's cause and elleswhere.

Parallels are constantly being drawn by Genius between ethical conduct in affairs of the heart and ethical conduct in general. In Book One Genius tells the tale of Mundus and Paulina to illustrate how Mundus, a lover who put aside reason in loving another man's wife, soon came to grief: 'For Love put Reson aweye / And can noght se the righte weye'. In Book Two we are told that whoever wishes to live virtuously must be governed not by blind passion but by reason.

> Nou understond, my sone and se,
> Ther is phisique for the seke,
> And vertus for the vices eke.
> Who that the vices wolde eshuie,
> He mot be Resoun thanne suie
> The vertus;

The appeal to the rational faculty in directing one's moral behaviour keeps wilfulness at bay and vice in retreat. The education of Amans has a direct bearing on the virtuous living of each individual: the pursuit of individual virtue within a social framework points the way to a morally ordered and peacefully united nation. Civic virtue is Gower's answer to the troubles of late fourteenth-century England, and it is a view no less powerfully conveyed for being conventional in fourteenth-century thought. It is the message of a particular age seeking, like all ages, peace and security in a troubled world.

For a modern reader the clearly-defined structure and thematic coherence of the *Confessio* may well be obscured by the very length and encyclopaedic spread of the poem. One is inclined to sympathize when C. S. Lewis complains that Gower 'says too much' (p.222). The *Confessio* is over 34,000 lines long, and the thematic coherence is not matched by a poetic unity. Yet the *Confessio* is much less tedious to read than might be expected from a poem of such length, and this is due in no small measure to the engaging personality of Amans. The instruction of Amans in the *Confessio* takes the form of a voyage of self-discvovery. The very act of confession functions as such. It is for Amans what would be regarded in modern psychological terminology as a process of analysis, a probing of one's personal life to ascertain the why's and wherefore's of certain behavioural patterns (see Peck (1978) pp. 30-33). In confessing his feelings and actions as a lover Amans provides us with a beautifully candid portrait of the pains and pleasures, the hopes and anxieties to which lovers are susceptible. When Amans is given the chance of leading his lady into chapel

> Thanne is noght al my weye in vein,
> Somdiel I may the betre fare,
> Whan I, that may noght fiele hir bare,
> May lede hire clothed in myn arm:
> Bot afterward it doth me harm
> Of pure imaginacioun;
> For thanne this collacioun
> I make unto myselven ofte,
> And seye, 'Ha lord, hou she is softe,
> How she is round, hou she is smal!
> Now wolde God I hadde hire al
> Withoute Danger at my wille!

Given the opportunity to spend time in the company of his lady and to accompany her in the dance is more than sufficient cause for pleasure.

> That whanne hir list on nihtes wake
> In chambre as to carole and daunce,
> Me thenkth I may ne more avaunce,
> If I may gon upon hir hond,
> Thanne if I wonne a kinges lond.
> For whanne I may hire hand beclippe
> With such gladnesse I daunce and skippe,
> Me thenkth I touche noght the flor;

There is a tone of delight here in remembering innocent pleasures, but there is also in the very telling a rueful recognition of the disparity between the joy felt and the pleasures enjoyed.

A note of rueful self-mockery is present when Amans describes how his reluctance to leave his lady's company leads him to resort to subterfuge:

> I take leve, and if I shal,
> I kisse hire, and go forth withal.
> And otherwhile, if that I dore,
> Er I come fully to the dore,
> I torne ayein and feigne a thing,
> As thogh I hadde lost a ring
> Or somewhat elles, for I wolde
> Kisse hire eftsones, if I sholde,
> Bot selden is that I so spede.

And when he is in bed, alone,

> Into hire bedd myn herte goth,
> And softly takth hire in his arm
> And fieleth hou that she is warm,
> And wisheth that his body were
> To fiele that he fieleth there.
> And thus myselven I tormente,
> Til that the dede slep me hente:
> Bot thanne be a thousand score
> Welmore that I was tofore

13

> I am tormented in my slep,
>
> Bot that I dreme is noght of shep:

Amans is well-aware that his lady does not love him, but he is a prisoner of his emotions and unable to disentangle himself.

> For ofte time she me bit
>
> To leven hire and chese a newe
>
> And seith, if I the sothe knewe
>
> How ferr I stonde from hir grace,
>
> I sholde love in other place.
>
> Bot therof woll I desobeye;
>
> For also wel she mihte seye,
>
> 'Go take the mone ther it sit';
>
> As bringe that into my wit:

The direct and lively tone in which Amans reveals his thoughts and actions is maintained in his exchanges with his confessor Genius. 'My wo to you is bot a game / That fielen noght of that I fiele' protests Amans. Displaying a very human trait Amans is reluctant at times to face facts and liable on occasion to query or protest at the advice Genius proffers. Humour is clearly present when Genius relates how Daphne was transformed into a laurel because of the over-hastiness in love of Phebus, and Amans responds to this cautionary tale by declaring that as long as 'I se my lady is / No tre, but halt hire oghne forme' he will continue to love her. More poignantly, when Genius advises Amans to avoid the sin of idleness Amans points out that his 'besinesse' in love has not been rewarded. 'The more that I knele and preye / With goode wordes and with softe / The more I am refused ofte'. And when Genius warns Amans against the sin of ingratitude he is in turn challenged to explain why that very charge should not be levelled instead at the disdainful lady 'for whom I soffre peine'. It is left to Genius to suggest that the love Amans feels for the lady 'Thogh it brenne evere as doth the fyr' is possibly inappropriate, governed as it is more by passion than by reason.

The authority to pronounce on matters of love is vested in Genius by Venus, goddess of Love, but Genius himself has literary precursors

14

in two well-known medieval texts, the *De Planctu Naturae* and the *Roman de la Rose*. In the *Roman* Genius is Nature's priest and seems to be associated with the procreative impulse through which the human race is perpetuated. Gower, however, disregards this specific association of Genius with procreation and assigns to him a wider tutelary role. In the *Confessio* Genius acknowledges God as ultimately responsible for 'the lawe of kinde' and sees 'kinde' itself, under the direct rule of Nature, as natural feeling. But natural feeling is inadequate without a moral basis and the 'lawe of kinde' can be disastrous when moral law is flouted. It is natural, for example, that feelings of love should stir in adolescence, but when moral law is abrogated and the will uncontrolled by reason disaster can result. Genius tells the tale of Canace and Machaire as an extreme illustration of such disaster.

> In chambre they togedre wone
> And as they sholden pleyde hem ofte,
> Til they be growen up alofte
> Into the youthe of lusty age,
> Whan kinde assaileth the corage
> With love and doth him forto bowe,
> That he no reson can allowe,
> Bot halt the lawe of nature:
>
> . . .
>
> As they al day togedre duelle,
> This brother mihte it noght asterte
> That he with al his hole herte
> His love upon his soster caste:

The delineation of a physical world within which the law of nature operates ideally in conjunction with moral law has its literary source in the *De Planctu Naturae*, and in his role as moral guide Genius follows in the footsteps of his literary predecessor in the *De Planctu*. But the role of Genius in the *Confessio* is more complex. As the priest of Venus he must concern himself with love, but within the confessional framework of the poem he acts as a father-confessor

15

adjudging all aspects of human behaviour, including love, according to the Christian code of morality. His teaching centres round the Seven Deadly Sins and the many tales he tells embody moral lessons relevant to the whole range of human conduct.

The tales provide entertainment as well as moral instruction, and Gower's skill at story-telling enables him to combine both. Not that this skill extends to all the stories he tells; a substantial number of them are simply dull—versified exempla. But where Gower's imagination is fully engaged the result is some excellent poetry. Gower's chief source for the stories Genius relates is Ovid, particularly the *Metamorphoses*, but he constantly streamlines Ovid's material, 'cutting the antique moorings and isolating the tellable tale' (Pearsall (1969) p. 20). What also emerges is a reinterpretation of the original stories in order to illustrate the moral truths with which Genius is concerned. Yet this is not done at the expense of the storyline. Gower concentrates on actions and events which embody in themselves moral significance. Within a tightly-knit, fast-moving narrative structure each story shows moral or immoral behaviour in action. Thus in Book One Florent's acceptance of marriage to an old hag who has saved his life illustrates the importance of upholding one's honour by keeping one's word in the face of adversity. The rape of Philomena by Tereus in Book Five enacts one outcome of blind passion, and reveals how it can set off an irrevocable train of events in which horror begets horror.

Characterization and visual imagery are rare, but descriptive detail can be used to powerful effect, as in the scene where Tereus seizes Philomena:

> And so that tyrant raviner,
> Whan that she was in his pouer,
> And he thereto saw time and place,
> As he that lost hath alle grace,
> Foryat he was a wedded man,
> And in a rage on hire he ran,
> Riht as a wolf which takth his preye.

And she began to crye and preye,
'O fader, o my moder diere,
Nou help!' Bot they ne mihte it hiere,
And she was of to litel miht
Defense ayein so ruide a kniht
To make, whanne he was so wod
That he no reson understod,
Bot hield hire under in such wise,
That she ne mihte noght arise,
Bot lay oppressed and desesed
As if a goshauk hadde sesed
A brid, which dorst noght for fere
Remue:

In Book Four the love of Pygmalion for a beautiful statue he has
sculpted expresses itself humorously but also poignantly through
his treatment of the statue as human, a wishfulness which only
increases his sexual frustration.

And after, whan the niht was come,
He leide hire in his bed al nakid.
He was forwept, he was forwakid,
He keste hire colde lippes ofte
And wisheth that they weren softe,
And ofte he rouncth in hire ere,
And ofte his arm now hier now there
He leide, as he hir wolde embrace,
And evere among he axeth grace,
As thogh she wiste what he mente:
And thus himself he gan tormente
With such desese of loves peine,
Than noman mihte him more peine.

And in Book Five the obsessive watchfulness of a jealous husband is
vividly portrayed:

This fiever is thanne of comun wone
Most grevous in a mannes yhe:

17

For thanne he makth him tote and pryhe,
Wher so as evere his love go;
She shal noght with hir litel too
Misteppe, bot he se it al.
His yhe is walkende overal;
Wher that she singe or that she dance,
He seth the leste contienance,
If she loke on a man aside
Or with him roune at eny tide,
Or that she lawghe, or that she loure,
His yhe is ther at every houre.

It is noticeable that in all three of the above extracts embellishment of diction and style play little part in the effectiveness of the narrative. Gower's use of the plain but apt word and an unadorned but fluent style is artistically at one with his flexible handling of the octosyllabic couplet. The very naturalness and unassuming nature of Gower's verse is a deliberate poetic choice, for as he says himself 'Of what matiere it shal be told / A tale lyketh manyfold / the betre, if it be spoke plein'. The very plainness and straightforwardness of the style concentrates the attention on the narrative itself, giving to the stories an immediacy of approach and appeal. The effectiveness of many of Gower's tales lies in the imaginative visualization of human behaviour at its best or worst, with sympathy and understanding accorded to the human predicament. But as Derek Pearsall notes, 'it is an imagination in which moral discrimination continues to operate, but operates in an artistically integrated manner' (1968, p. 477). Virtuous action is the end to which we are being directed, and if the stories are entertaining they are also, and primarily, instructive.

Within the confessional framework Amans sees his thoughts and actions reflected back at him, but through a moral lens, and it is by means of an actual mirror that his final release from the snares of passion is effected. In a passage which has been described as 'one of the most haunting pieces of writing in medieval English' (Gray, p. 319), Venus makes Amans look at himself in a mirror. Amans sees his 'yhen dimme', his 'chiekes thinne', his 'heres hore', and his whole face wrinkled with age. 'My will was tho to se nomore', he sadly acknowledges. But facing in the mirror the irrefutable evidence of his old age brings with it the final acceptance of his unsuitability as a lover. Instead, as Venus bids him, he will go 'ther vertu moral duelleth', and through his books 'besieche and preye hierafter for the pes'. Venus takes her leave and Amans, released from the torments of passion, goes 'homward a softe pas'. Henceforth he will pursue a different labour of love: the promotion, through his role as poet, of communal peace and harmony. Thus we return, as we began, to Gower the poet.

In the *Confessio* Gower draws an analogy between Amans, an old man in need of moral instruction, and the world, growing old in time and in need of moral reform. In his Prologue Gower contrasts the 'tyme passed' when 'the world stod thanne in al his welthe' with the discordant present in which 'justice out of the weye / With rihtwisness is gone aweye'. The closing section of the poem, framed as an epilogue, returns the audience to the wider issue of social harmony and peace within the troubled England of the 1390's. The *Confessio* ends with a prayer to God that 'He this lond in siker weye / Wol sette uppon good governance'. The way forward, as Gower sees it, is not through that self-regarding and self-seeking love which pursues singular profit above everything and everyone else, but that virtuous and unselfish love which expresses itself in concern for the welfare of the community at large. Although by conscious choice a moralist rather than an entertainer, Gower recognized the need to combine instruction with delight. This edition of extracts from the *Confessio Amantis* will, I hope, introduce readers to some of the delights of an undeservedly neglected medieval poet.

TEXTUAL NOTE

Of the eight books of the *Confessio Amantis* extracts from six are included in the present selection. Those parts of the poem which have been entirely omitted are the Prologue, Book Two, and Book Seven.

The text of the selections is based on the edition of the poem by G. C. Macaulay, vols. II and III in *The Complete Works of John Gower*, Oxford, 1901. Macaulay based his text on Bodleian MS. Fairfax 3, a copy of the third version of the poem, and regarded as the most authoritative of over forty manuscripts of the poem which have survived. The manuscripts are discussed by Macaulay in vol. II, intro. cxxvii-clxvii, and, more recently, by John Fisher in *John Gower*, London, 1965, pp. 116-27.

For greater ease of reading Gower's poetry a few minor changes have been made to Macaulay's text. The spelling *sch* has been modernized to *sh*, and the use of *i/y* regularized where necessary to bring it into line with modern usage. Macaulay modernized the punctuation in his edition, but left the system of capitalization unchanged. In this edition the system of capitalization has been revised to make it conform, as far as possible, to modern practice. A difficulty arises in that Gower treats the various subdivisions of the Seven Deadly Sins as characters in their own right; capitalization is used, thus, when referring to them. Where love is personified in the poem it is also capitalized.

GLOSSES

Words likely to cause difficulty are glossed in the text so as to facilitate the reading of the poem. Phrases, and lines of poetry which need explaining are, as a rule, rendered into modern English in the notes. Glossed words repeated in the immediate context are not re-glossed. The words listed below are frequently used, and not normally glossed in the text itself:

ayein: again, against
ek(e): also
hor(e): her
mot(e): must
noght: not, nothing
oghne/oughne: own
than(ne): then
wiht: person, creature
wot: know(s)
yive: give

be: by
er: before
her(e): their
nam: took
not: know(s) not
ous: us
tho: then, those
wiste: knew
yhe: eye

bot: but, unless, only
fro: from
hem: them
nih: near
o/on: one
sih(e)/sigh: saw
whan(ne): when
wole/wol(l): will
yit: yet

SELECT BIBLIOGRAPHY

EDITIONS

The Complete Works of John Gower, ed. G. C. Macaulay, Oxford, 1901, 4 vols.

Selections from John Gower, ed. J. A. W. Bennett (Clarendon Medieval and Tudor Series), Oxford, 1968.

Confessio Amantis, ed. R. A. Peck, New York, 1968.

STUDIES

Baker, D. N., 'The Priesthood of Genius: A Study of the Medieval Tradition', *Speculum* 51 (1976), pp. 277-91.

Bennett, J. A. W., 'Gower's *Honeste Love*' in *Patterns of Love and Courtesy: Essays in Memory of C. S. Lewis*, ed. John Lawlor, London, 1966, pp. 107-21.

Burrow, J. A., *Ricardian Poetry: Chaucer, Gower, Langland and the 'Gawain' Poet*, London, 1971.

Dean, James, 'Time Past and Time Present in Chaucer's *Clerk's Tale* and Gower's *Confessio Amantis*', *English Literary History* 44 (1977), pp. 401-18.

Economou, G. D., 'The Character Genius in Alain de Lille, Jean de Meun, and John Gower', *Chaucer Review* 4 (1970/71), pp. 203-10.

Ferguson, A. B., *The Articulate Citizen and the English Renaissance*, Duke Univ. Press, 1965.

Fisher, J. H., *John Gower: Moral Philosopher and Friend of Chaucer*, London, 1965.

Fison, P., 'The Poet in John Gower', *Essays in Criticism*, 8 (1958), pp. 16-26.

Gallacher, P. J., *Love, the Word, and Mercury: A Reading of Gower's 'Confessio Amantis'*, Univ. of New Mexico Press, 1975.

Gilroy-Scott, N. W., 'John Gower's Reputation: Literary Allusions from the early Fifteenth Century to the Time of *Pericles*', *The Yearbook of English Studies* 1 (1971), pp. 30-47.

Gray, Douglas, 'Later Poetry: The Courtly Tradition' in *The Middle Ages*, ed. W. F. Bolton, *Sphere History of Literature in the English Language*, vol. 1, London, 1970, pp. 312-370.

Lawlor, John, 'On Romanticism in the *Confessio Amantis*' in *Patterns of Love and Courtesy*, ed. John Lawlor, London, 1966, pp. 122-140.

Lewis, C. S. *The Allegory of Love: A Study in Medieval Tradition*, Oxford Univ. Press, 1936.

Mainzer, Conrad, 'John Gower's Use of the Medieval Ovid in *Confessio Amantis*', *Medium Aevum* 41 (1972), pp. 215-29.

Middleton, Anne, 'The Idea of Public Poetry in the Reign of Richard II', *Speculum* 53 (1978), pp. 94-114.

Pantin, W. A., *The English Church in the Fourteenth Century*, Cambridge, 1955.

Pearsall, Derek, 'Gower's Narrative Art', *Publications of the Modern Language Association of America* 81 (1966), pp. 475-84.

Pearsall, Derek, *Gower and Lydgate*, Writers and Their Work: No. 211, Longmans, 1969.

Peck, R. A. *Kingship & Common Profit in Gower's 'Confessio Amantis'*, Southern Illinois Univ. Press, 1978.

Schmidt, Michael, 'John Gower' in *An Introduction to 50 British Poets 1300-1900* (Pan Literature Guides), London and Sydney, 1979, pp. 13-22.

Schueler, D. G., 'Gower's Characterization of Genius in the *Confessio Amantis*', *Modern Language Quarterly* 33 (1972), pp. 240-256.

Woolf, Rosemary, 'Moral Chaucer and Kindly Gower' in *J. R. R. Tolkien, Scholar and Storyteller*, ed. Mary Salu and R. T. Farrell, Cornell Univ. Pres, 1979, pp. 221-248.

OED: The Oxford English Dictionary, ed. Sir J. A. H. Murray, H. Bradley, Sir W. Craigie, C. T. Onions, Oxford, 1933.

Middle English Dictionary, ed. H. Kurath and S. M. Kuhn, University of Michigan Press, 1954—.

BOOK ONE

Amans:

I may noght strecche up to the hevene
Myn hand, ne setten al in evene
This world, which evere is in balance: uncertainty
It stant noght in my sufficance   ability
So grete thinges to compasse,
Bot I mot lete it overpasse
And treten upon othre thinges.
Forthy the stile of my writinges
Fro this day forth I thenke change
And speke of thing is noght so strange,   (10)
Which every kinde hath upon honde,
And wherupon the world mot stonde,
And hath don sithen it began,
And shal whil ther is any man;
And that is Love, of which I mene
To trete, as after shal be sene.
In which ther can noman him reule,
For Loves lawe is out of reule,
That of tomoche or of tolite
Welnih is every man to wite,   be blamed
And natheles ther is noman   (21)
In al this world so wis, that can
Of Love tempre the mesure,
Bot as it falth in aventure: by chance
For wit ne strengthe may noght helpe,
And he which elles wolde him yelpe   boast
Is rathest throwen under fote,   quickest
Ther can no wiht therof do bote.   have help
For yet was nevere such covine,   secret art
That couthe ordeine a medicine   (30)
To thing which God in lawe of kinde

Hath set, for ther may noman finde
The rihte salve of such a sor.
It hath and shal ben everemor
That Love is maister wher he wile,
Ther can no lif make other skile;
For wher as evere him lest to sette,   he desires
Ther is no miht which him may lette.   prevent
Bot what shal fallen ate laste,
The sothe can no wisdom caste,   the truth
Bot as it falleth upon chance;   (41)
For if ther evere was balance
Which of Fortune stant governed,
I may wel lieve as I am lerned   believe
That Love hath that balance on honde,
Which wol no Reson understonde.
For Love is blind and may noght se,
Forthy may no certeinete
Be set upon his jugement,
Bot as the whiel aboute went   (50)
He yifth his graces undeserved,
And fro that man which hath him served
Fulofte he takth aweye his fees,
As he that pleyeth ate dees,   dice
And therupon what shal befalle
He not, til that the chance falle,
Wher he shal lese or he shal winne.
And thus fulofte men beginne,
That if they wisten what it mente,   knew
They wolde change al here entente.   (60)
     And forto proven it is so,
I am myselven on of tho,
Which to this scole am underfonge.   received
For it is sithe go noght longe,
As forto speke of this matiere,

26

I may you telle, if ye woll hiere,
A wonder hap which me befell,
That was to me bothe hard and fell,   cruel
Touchende of Love and his fortune,
The which me liketh to comune   talk about
And pleinly forto telle it oute.   (71)
To hem that ben lovers aboute
Fro point to point I wol declare
And writen of my woful care,
My wofull day, my wofull chance,
That men mowe take remembrance   may
Of that they shall hierafter rede:
For in good feith this wolde I rede,   advise
That every man ensample take   (79)
Of wisdom which him is betake,   is allotted to
And that he wot of good aprise   instruction
To teche it forth, for such emprise   enterprise
Is forto preise; and therfore I
Woll write and shewe al openly
How Love and I togedre mette,
Wherof the world ensample fette   take
May after this, whan I am go,
Of thilke unsely jolit wo,   unhappy
Whos reule stant out of the weye,
Nou glad and nou gladnesse aweye,   (90)
And yet it may noght be withstonde
For oght that men may understonde.

Upon the point that is befalle
Of love, in which that I am falle,
I thenke telle my matiere:
Now herkne, who that wol it hiere,
Of my fortune how that it ferde.
This enderday, as I forthferde   other day

27

To walke, as I yow telle may,—
And that was in the monthe of May,   (100)
Whan every brid hath chose his make   mate
And thenkth his merthes forto make
Of love that he hath achieved;
Bot so was I nothing relieved,
For I was further fro my love
Than erthe is fro the hevene above,
As forto speke of eny sped:
So wiste I me no other red,   counsel
Bot as it were a man forfare   worn out
Unto the wode I gan to fare,   (110)
Noght forto singe with the briddes,
For whanne I was the wode amiddes,
I fond a swote grene pleine,
And ther I gan my wo compleigne
Wishinge and wepinge al myn one,   alone
For other merthes made I none.
So hard me was that ilke throwe,   selfsame pain
That ofte sithes overthrowe
To grounde I was withoute breth;
And ever I wishide after deth,   (120)
Whanne I out of my peine awok,
And caste up many a pitous lok
Unto the hevene, and seide thus:
'O thou Cupide, O thou Venus,
Thou god of Love and thou goddesse,
Wher is pite? wher is meknesse?
Now doth me pleinly live or die,
For certes such a maladye
As I now have and longe have hadd,
It mihte make a wisman madd,   (130)
If that it sholde longe endure.
O Venus, queene of loves cure,

Thou lif, thou lust, thou mannes hele,   pleasure; salvation
Behold mý cause and my querele,
And yif me som part of thy grace,
So that I may finde in this place
If thou be gracious or non.'
And with that word I sawh anon
The king of Love and qweene bothe;
Bot he that king with yhen wrothe   (140)
His chiere aweyward fro me caste,   face
And forth he passede ate laste.
Bot natheles er he forth wente
A firy dart me thoghte he hente   seized
And threw is thurgh myn herte rote:
In him fond I no other bote,   relief
For lenger list him noght to duelle.
Bot she that is the source and welle
Of wel or wo, that shal betide   (149)
To hem that loven, at that tide   time
Abod, bot forto tellen hiere   stayed
She cast on me no goodly chiere:
Thus natheles to me she seide,
'What art thou, sone?' and I abreide   started up
Riht as a man doth out of slep,
And therof tok she riht good kep
And bad me nothing ben adrad: not to be afraid
Bot for al that I was noght glad,
For I ne sawh no cause why.   (159)
And eft she asketh, what was I: then
I seide, 'A caitif that lith hiere: wretch
What wolde ye, my lady diere?
Shal I ben hol or elles die?'
She seide, 'Tell thy maladye:
What is thy sor of which thou pleignest?
Ne hid it noght, for if thou feignest,

29

I can do the no medicine.'
'Ma dame, I am a man of thine,
That in thy court have longe served,
And aske that I have deserved,   (170)
Som wele after my longe wo.'
And she began to loure tho,   frown
And seide, 'Ther is manye of yow
Faitours, and so may be that thow   deceivers
Art riht such on, and be feintise   pretence
Seist that thou hast me do servise.'
And natheles she wiste wel,
My world stod on an other whiel
Withouten eny faiterye: (179)
Bot algate of my maladye   in any case
She bad me telle and seye hir trowthe.
'Ma dame, if ye wolde have rowthe,'
Quod I, 'than wolde I telle yow.'
'Sey forth,' quod she, 'and tell me how;
Shew me thy seknesse everydiel.'
'Ma dame, that can I do wel,
Be so my lif therto wol laste.'
With that hir lok on me she caste,
And seide: 'In aunter if thou live,   in case
My will is ferst that thou be shrive;   (190)
And natheles how that it is
I wot myself, bot for al this
Unto my prest, which comth anon,
I woll thou telle it on and on,   point by point
Bothe all thy thoght and al thy werk.
O Genius myn oghne clerk,
Com forth and hier this mannes shrifte,'
Quod Venus tho; and I uplifte
Myn hed with that, and gan beholde
The selve prest, which as she wolde   (200)

Was redy there and sette him doun
To hiere my confessioun.

   This worthy prest, this holy man
To me spekende thus began,
And seide: 'Benedicite,
My sone, of the felicite
Of love and ek of all the wo
Thou shalt thee shrive of bothe tuo.
What thou er this for loves sake
Hast felt, let nothing be forsake,   (210)
Tell pleinliche as it is befalle.'
And with that word I gan doun falle
On knees, and with devocioun
And with full gret contricioun
I seide thanne; 'Dominus,
Myn holy fader Genius,
So as thou hast experience
Of Love, for whos reverence
Thou shalt me shriven at this time,
I pray the let me noght mistime   (220)
My shrifte, for I am destourbed
In al myn herte, and so contourbed,   perturbed
That I ne may my wittes gete,
So shal I moche thing foryete:
Bot if thou wolt my shrifte oppose   question
Fro point to point, thanne I suppose,
Ther shal nothing be left behinde.
Bot now my wittes ben so blinde,
That I ne can myselven teche.'
Tho he began anon to preche,   (230)
And with his wordes debonaire   kindly
He seide tome softe and faire:
'Thy shrifte to oppose and hiere,

31

My sone, I am assigned hiere
Be Venus the godesse above,
Whos prest I am touchende of Love.
Bot natheles for certein skile
I mot algate and nedes wile   assuredly
Noght only make my spekinges
Of Love, bot of othre thinges,   (240)
That touchen to the cause of vice.
For that belongeth to thoffice
Of prest, whos ordre that I bere,
So that I wol nothing forbere,
That I the vices on and on   one by one
Ne shal thee shewen everychon;
Wherof thou miht take evidence
To reule with thy conscience.
Bot of conclusion final
Conclude I wol in special   (250)
For Love, whos servant I am,
And why the cause is that I cam.
So thenke I to don bothe tuo,
Ferst that myn ordre longeth to,
The vices forto telle arewe,   in due order
Bot next above alle othre shewe
Of Love I wol the propretes,
How that they stonde be degrees
After the disposicioun
Of Venus, whos condicioun   (260)
I moste folwe, as I am holde.   obliged
For I with Love am al withholde,   in service
So that the lasse I am to wite,   be blamed
Thogh I ne conne bot a lite   know
Of othre thinges that ben wise:
I am noght tawht in such a wise;
For it is noght my comun us   customary practice

32

To speke of vices and vertus,
Bot al of Love and of his lore,   teaching
For Venus bokes of nomore   (270)
Me techen nowther text ne glose.   commentary
Bot for als moche as I suppose
It sit a prest to be wel thewed,   befits; instructed
And shame it is if he be lewed,   unlearned
Of my presthode after the forme
I wol thy shrifte so enforme,
That ate leste thou shalt hiere
The vices and to thy matiere
Of love I shal hem so remene,   relate
That thou shalt knowe what they mene.   (280)
For what a man shal axe or sein
Touchende of shrifte, it mot be plein,
It nedeth noght to make it queinte,   refine upon it
For Trowthe hise wordes wol noght peinte:
That I wole axe of the forthy,
My sone, it shal be so pleinly,
That thou shalt knowe and understonde
The pointz of shrifte how that they stonde.'

   Between the lif and deth I herde
This prestes tale er I answerde,   (290)
And thanne I preide him forto seye
His will, and I it wolde obeye
After the forme of his apprise.   teaching
Tho spake he tome in such a wise,
And bad me that I sholde shrive
As touchende of my wittes five,   senses
And shape that they were amended
Of that I hadde hem misdispended.
For tho be proprely the gates,
Thurgh whiche as to the herte algates   (300)

33

Comth alle thing unto the feire,
Which may the mannes soule empeire.
And now this matiere is broght inne,
My sone, I thenke ferst beginne
To wite how that thin yhe hath stonde,   find out
The which is, as I understonde,
The moste principal of alle,
Thurgh whom that peril may befalle.
   And forto speke in Loves kinde,
Ful manye suche a man may finde,   (310)
Whiche evere caste aboute here yhe,
To loke if that they mihte aspye
Fulofte thing which hem ne toucheth,
Bot only that here herte soucheth   suspects
In hindringe of an other wiht;
And thus ful may a worthy kniht
And many a lusty lady bothe
Have be fulofte sithe wrothe.   very often
So that an yhe is as a thief
To love, and doth ful gret meschief;   (320)
And also for his oghne part
Fulofte thilke firy dart
Of Love, which that evere brenneth,
Thurgh him into the herte renneth:
And thus a mannes yhe ferst
Himselve grieveth alther werst,   worst of all
And many a time that he knoweth
Unto his oghne harm it groweth.
My sone, herkne now forthy
A tale, to be war therby   (330)
Thin yhe forto kepe and warde,
So that it passe noght his warde.

*   *   *

*　　*　　*

    This vice of Inobedience
Ayein the reule of conscience
Al that is humble he desalloweth,
That he toward his God ne boweth
After the lawes of His heste.   command
Noght as a man bot as a beste,
Which goth upon his lustes wilde,
So goth this proude vice unmilde,   (340)
That he desdeigneth alle lawe:
He not what is to be felawe,
And serve may he noght for pride;
So is he badde on every side,
And is that selve of whom men speke,
Which wol noght bowe er that he breke.
I not if Love him mihte plye,   bend
For elles forto justefye
His herte, I not what mihte availe.   (349)

Confessor:
Forthy, my sone, of such entaile   fashion
If that thin herte be disposed,
Tell out and let it noght be glosed: concealed
For if that thou unbuxom be   disobedient
To Love, I not in what degree
Thou shalt thy goode world achieve.

Amans:
My fader, ye shul wel believe,
The yonge whelp which is affaited   trained
Hath noght his maister betre awaited,
To couche, whan he seith 'Go lowe,'
That I, anon as I may knowe   (360)

35

My lady will, ne bowe more.
Bot other while I grucche sore   complain
Of some thinges that she doth,
Wherof that I woll telle soth:
For of tuo pointz I am bethoght,
That, thogh I wolde, I mihte noght
Obeye unto my lady heste;
Bot I dar make this beheste,   promise
Save only of that ilke tuo   same
I am unbuxom of no mo.   (370)

C: What ben tho tuo? tell on, quod he.

A: My fader, this is on, that she
Commandeth me my mowth to close,
And that I sholde hir noght oppose
In love, of which I ofte preche,
Bot plenerliche of such a speche   fully
Forbere, and soffren hire in pes.
Bot that ne mihte I natheles
For al this world obeye iwiss;   certainly
For whanne I am ther as she is,   (380)
Though she my tales noght alowe,
Ayein hir will yit mot I bowe,
To seche if that I mihte have grace:
Bot that thing may I noght enbrace
For ought that I can speke or do;
And yit fulofte I speke so,
That she is wroth and seith, 'Be stille.'
If I that heste shal fulfille
And therto ben obedient,   (389)
Thanne is my cause fully shent,   harmed
For specheles may noman spede.
So wot I noght what is to rede;   is advisable

Bot certes I may noght obeye,
That I ne mot algate seye   in any event
Somwhat of that I wolde mene;
For evere it is aliche grene,   similarly
The grete love which I have,
Wherof I can noght bothe save
My speche and this obedience:
And thus fulofte my silence   (400)
I breke, and is the ferste point
Wherof that I am out of point
In this, and yit it is no pride.
    Now thanne upon that other side
To telle my desobeissance,
Ful sore it stant to my grevance
And may noght sinke into my wit;
For ofte time she me bit
To leven hire and chese a newe,
And seith, if I the sothe knewe   (410)
How ferr I stonde from hir grace,
I sholde love in other place.
Bot therof woll I desobeye;
For also wel she mihte seye,
'Go tak the mone ther it sit,'
As bringe that into my wit:
For ther was nevere rooted tre,
That stod so faste in his degre,
That I ne stonde more faste
Upon hire love, and may noght caste   (420)
Myn herte awey, althogh I wolde.
For God wot, thogh I never sholde
Sen hir with yhe after this day,
Yit stant it so that I ne may
Hir love out of my brest remue.
This is a wonder retenue,   wondrous service

That malgre wher she wole or non   *despite*
Myn herte is everemore in on,   *on one*
So that I can non other chese,
Bot whether that I winne or lese,   (430)
I moste hire loven til I deie;
And thus I breke as be that weye
Hire hestes and hir commandinges,
Bot trewliche in non othre thinges.
Forthy, my fadre, what is more
Touchende to this ilke lore   *some teaching*
I you beseche, after the forme
That ye pleinly me wolde enforme,
So that I may myn herte reule
In loves cause after the reule.   (440)

C: Toward this vice of which we trete
Ther ben yit tweie of thilke estrete,   *kind*
Here name is Murmur and Compleignte:
Ther can noman here chiere peinte,   *face*
To sette a glad semblant therinne,   *expression*
For thogh Fortune make hem winne,
Yit grucchen they, and if they lese,   *complain*
Ther is no weye forto chese,
Wherof they mihten stonde appesed.   (449)
So ben they comunly desesed;   *jointly*
Ther may no welthe ne poverte
Attempren hem to the decerte   *temper; virtue*
Of buxomnesse be no wise: *obedience*
For ofte time they despise
The goode fortune as the badde,
As they no mannes reson hadde,
Thurgh pride, wherof they be blinde.
     And riht of such a maner kinde

Ther be lovers, that thogh they have
Of love al that they wolde crave,   (460)
Yit wol they grucche be som weye,
That they wol noght to Love obeye
Upon the trowthe, as they do sholde;
And if hem lacketh that they wolde,
Anon they falle in such a peine,
That evere unbuxomly they pleigne
Upon Fortune, and curse and crye,
That they wol noght here hertes plye   bend
To soffre til it betre falle.
Forthy if thou amonges alle   (470)
Hast used this condicioun,
My sone, in thy confessioun
Now tell me pleinly what thou art.

A: My fader, I beknowe a part,   confess
So as ye tolden hier above
Of murmur and compleignte of love,
That for I se no sped comende,
Ayein fortune compleignende
I am, as who seith, evermo:
And ek fulofte time also,   (480)
Whan so is that I se and hiere
Or hevy word or hevy chiere
Of my lady, I grucche anon;
Bot wordes dar I speke non,
Wherof she mihte be desplesed,
Bot in myn herte I am desesed:
With many a murmur, God it wot,
Thus drinke I in myn oghne swot,   sweat
And thogh I make no semblant,   show
Myn herte is al desobeissant;   (490)
And in this wise I me confesse

39

Of that ye clepe unbuxomnesse.   call
Now telleth what youre counseil is.

C: My sone, and I thee rede this,   advise
What so befalle of other weye,
That thou to Loves heste obeye
Als ferr as thou it miht suffise:
For ofte sithe in such a wise   often
Obedience in love availeth,
Wher al a mannes strengthe faileth;   (500)
Wherof if that the list to wite   you wish to know
In a Cronique as it is write,
A gret ensample thou miht finde,
Which now is come to my minde.

    Ther was whilom be dayes olde
A worthy kniht, and as men tolde
He was nevoeu to themperour
And of his court a courteour:
Wifles he was, Florent he hihte,   was called
He was a man that mochel mihte,   (510)
Of armes he was desirous,
Chivalerous and amorous,
And for the fame of worldes speche,
Strange aventures forto seche,
He rod the Marches al aboute.   border territories
And fell a time, as he was oute,
Fortune, which may every thred
Tobreke, and knette of mannes sped,
Shop, as this kniht rod in a pas,   contrived
That he be strengthe take was,   (520)
And to a castell they him ladde,
Wher that he fewe frendes hadde:
For so it fell that ilke stounde   time

That he hath with a dedly wounde
Feihtende his oghne hondes slain | with his own
Branchus, which to the capitain
Was sone and heir, wherof ben wrothe
The fader and the moder bothe.
That kniht Branchus was of his hond | in valour
The worthieste of al his lond, | (530)
And fain they wolden do vengance
Upon Florent, bot remembrance
That they toke of his worthinesse
Of knihthod and of gentilesse,
And how he stod of cousinage
To themperour, made hem assuage,
And dorsten noght slen him for fere:
In gret desputeisoun they were
Among hemself, what was the beste.
Ther was a lady, the slyheste | (540)
Of alle that men knewe tho,
So old she mihte unethes go, | scarcely walk
And was grantdame unto the dede: | grandmother; dead man
And she with that began to rede,
And seide how she wol bringe him inne,
That she shal him to dethe winne
Al only of his oghne grant, | consent
Thurgh strengthe of verray covenant | proper agreement
Withoute blame of eny wiht.
Anon she sende for this kniht, | (550)
And of hire sone she alleide | accused
The deth, and thus to him she seide:
'Florent, how so thou be to wite | blame
Of Branchus deth, men shal respite | delay
As now to take vengement,
Be so thou stonde in juggement
Upon certein condicioun,

That thou unto a questioun
Which I shal axe shalt ansuere;
And over this thou shalt ek swere,   (560)
That if thou of the sothe faile,
Ther shal non other thing availe,
That thou ne shalt thy deth receive.
And for men shal thee noght deceive,
That thou therof miht ben avised,
Thou shalt have day and time assised   appointed
And leve saufly forto wende,
Be so that at thy dayes ende
Thou come ayein with thin avis.   opinion
    This kniht, which worthy was and wis,   (570)
This lady preith that he may wite,   know
And have it under seales write,
What questioun it sholde be
For which he shal in that degree
Stonde of his lif in jeupartye.
With that she feigneth compaignye,   friendship
And seith: 'Florent, on love it hongeth
Al that to myn axinge longeth:
What alle wommen most desire   (579)
This wole I axe, and in thempire   kingdom
Wher as thou hast most knowlechinge
Tak conseil upon this axinge.'
    Florent this thing hath undertake,
The day was set, the time take,
Under his seal he wrot his oth,
In such a wise and forth he goth
Hom to his emes court ayein;   uncle's
To whom his aventure plein
He tolde, of that him is befalle.
And upon that they weren alle   (590)
The wiseste of the lond asent,

Bot natheles of on assent
They mihte noght acorde plat,   plainly agree
On seide this, an othre that.
After the disposicioun   arrangement
Of naturel complexioun
To som womman it is plesance,
That to an other is grevance;
Bot such a thing in special,
Which to hem alle in general   (600)
Is most plesant, and most desired
Above alle othre and most conspired,   agreed upon
Such o thing conne they noght finde
Be constellacioun ne kinde:
And thus Florent withoute cure
Mot stonde upon his aventure,
And is al shape unto the lere,   destined; loss of life
As in defalte of his answere.
This kniht hath levere forto die
Than breke his trowthe and forto lie   (610)
In place ther as he was swore,
And shapth him gon ayein therfore.
Whan time cam he tok his leve,
That lengere wolde he noght beleve,   remain
And preith his em he be noght wroth,
For that is a point of his oth,
He seith, that noman shal him wreke,   avenge
Thogh afterward men hiere speke
That he par aventure deie.   by chance
And thus he wente forth his weye   (620)
Alone as kniht aventurous,
And in his thoght was curious   much exercised
To wite what was best to do:
And as he rod al one so,   thus alone
And cam nih ther he wolde be,

In a forest under a tre
He sih wher sat a creature,
A lothly wommanish figure,
That forto speke of fleish and bon
So foul yit sih he nevere non.   (630)
This kniht behield hir redely,   looked at; quickly
And as he wolde have passed by,
She cleped him and bad abide;
And he his horse heved aside   head
Tho torneth, and to hire he rod,
And there he hoveth and abod,
To wite what she wolde mene.
And she began him to bemene,   condole with
And seide: 'Florent be thy name,
Thou hast on honde such a game,   (640)
That bot thou be the betre avised,
Thy deth is shapen and devised,
That al the world ne may the save,
Bot if that thou my conseil have.'
    Florent, whan he this tale herde,
Unto this olde wiht answerede
And of hir conseil he hir preide.
And she ayein to him thus seide:
'Florent, if I for the so shape,
That thou thurgh me thy deth ascape   (650)
And take worshipe of thy dede,
What shal I have to my mede?'   reward
'What thing,' quod he, 'that thou wolt axe.'
'I bidde nevere a betre taxe,' ask for;   ask for; arrangement
Quod she, 'bot ferst, er thou be sped,   said
Thou shalt me leve such a wedd,   pledge
That I wol have thy trowthe in honde
That thou shalt be myn housebonde.'
'Nay,' seith Florent, 'that may noght be.'

44

'Rid thanne forth thy wey,'quod she, (660)
'And if thou go withoute red,
Thou shalt be sekerliche ded.' certainly
Florent behihte hire good inowh promised
Of londe, of rente, of park, of plowh,
Bot al that compteth she at noght. sets
Tho fell this kniht in mochel thoght,
Now goth he forth, now comth ayein,
He wot noght what is best to sein,
And thoghte, as he rod to and fro,
That chese he mot on of the tuo, (670)
Or forto take hire to his wif
Or elles forto lese his lif.
And thanne he caste his avantage,
That she was of so gret an age,
That she may live bot a while,
And thoghte put hire in an ile,
Wher that noman hire sholde knowe,
Til she with death were overthrowe.
And thus this yonge lusty kniht
Unto this olde lothly wiht (680)
Tho seide: 'If that non other chance
May make my deliverance,
Bot only thilke same speche
Which, as thou seist, thou shalt me teche,
Have hier myn hond, I shal thee wedde.'
And thus his trowthe he leith to wedde.
With that she frounceth up the browe; wrinkles
'This covenant I wol allowe,'
She seith: 'if eny other thing
Bot that thou hast of my teching (690)
Fro deth thy body may respite,
I woll thee of thy trowthe acquite,
And elles be non other weye.

45

Now herkne me what I shal seye.
Whan thou art come into the place,
Wher now they maken gret manace   threats
And upon thy cominge abide,
They wole anon the same tide   time
Oppose thee of thin answere.
I wot thou wolt nothing forbere   (700)
Of that thou wenest be thy beste,   think
And if thou miht so finde reste,
Wel is, for thanne is ther nomore.
And elles this shal be my lore,
That thou shalt seye upon this molde   earth
That alle wommen lievest wolde   most dearly
Be soverein of mannes love:
For what womman is so above,
She hath, as who seith, al hire wille;
And elles may she noght fulfille   (710)
What thing hir were lievest have.
With this answere thou shalt save
Thyself, and other wise noght.
And when thou hast thin ende wroght,
Com hier ayein, thou shalt me finde,
And let nothing out of thy minde.'

    He goth him forth with hevy chiere,
As he that not in what manere
He may this worldes joye atteigne:
For if he deie, he hath a peine,   (720)
And if he live, he mot him binde
To such on which of alle kinde
Of wommen is thunsemlieste:
Thus wot he noght what is the beste:
Bot be him lief or be him loth,
Unto the castell forth he goth
His full answere forto yive,

46

Or forto deie or forto live.
Forth with his conseil cam the lord,   council
The thinges stoden of record,   (730)
He sende up for the lady sone,
And forth she cam, that olde mone.   crone
In presence of the remenant
The strengthe of al the covenant
Tho was reherced openly,
And to Florent she bad forthy
That he shal tellen his avis,   opinion
As he that woot what is the pris.   knows
Florent seith al that evere he couthe,
Bot such word cam ther non to mowthe,   (740)
That he for yifte or for beheste   by gift; promise
Mihte eny wise his deth areste.
And thus he tarieth longe and late,
Til that this lady bad algate   nevertheless
That he shal for the dom final   judgement
Yive his answere in special
Of that she hadde him ferst opposed: questioned
And thanne he hath trewly supposed
That he him may of nothing yelpe,   boast
Bot if so be tho wordes helpe,   (750)
Whiche as the womman hath him tawht;
Wherof he hath an hope cawht
That he shal ben excused so,
And tolde out plein his wille tho.
And whan that this matrone herde
The manere how this kniht ansuerde,
She seide: 'Ha treson, wo thee be,
That hast thus told the privite,
Which alle wommen most desire!
I wolde that thou were afire.'   (760)
Bot natheles in such a plit

Florent of his answere is quit: *acquitted*
And tho began his sorwe newe,
For he mot gon, or ben untrewe,
To hire which his trowthe hadde.
Bot he, which alle shame dradde,
Goth forth in stede of his penance,   *to the place*
And takth the fortune of his chance,
As he that was with trowthe affaited.   *governed by*
    This olde wiht him hath awaited   *(770)*
In place wher as he hire lefte:
Florent his wofull heved uplefte
And sih this vecke wher she sat,   *hag*
Which was the lothlieste what   *thing*
That evere man caste on his yhe:
Hire nase bass, hire browes hihe,   *flat*
Hire yhen smale and depe set,
Hire chekes ben with teres wet,
And rivelen as an emty skin   *wrinkled*
Hangende doun unto the chin,   *(780)*
Hire lippes shrunken ben for age,
Ther was no grace in the visage,
Hir front was nargh, hir lockes hore, *forehead; narrow; hoary*
She loketh forth as doth a More,   *peers out; Moor*
Hire necke is short, hir shuldres courbe,   *bent*
That mihte a mannes lust destourbe,
Hire body gret and nothing smal,
And shortly to descrive hire al,
She hath no lith withoute a lak;   *limb; fault*
Bot lich unto the wollesak   *a sack of wool*
She proferth hire unto this kniht,   *(791)*
And bad him, as he hath behiht,
So as she hath ben his warant,
That he hire holde covenant,
And be the bridel she him seseth.

48

Bot Godd wot how that she him pleseth
Of suche wordes as she spekth:
Him thenkth welnih his herte brekth
For sorwe that he may noght fle,
Bot if he wolde untrewe be. (800)

    Loke, how a sek man for his hele
Takth baldemoine with canele, *gentian; cinnamon*
And with the myrre takth the sucre, *myrrh*
Riht upon such a maner lucre *lucre*
Stant Florent, as in this diete:
He drinkth the bitre with the swete,
He medleth sorwe with likinge,
And liveth, as who seith, deyinge;
His youthe shal be cast aweye (809)
Upon such on which as the weye *whey*
Is old and lothly overal.
Bot nede he mot that nede shal:
He wolde algate his trowthe holde,
As every kniht therto is holde,
What happ so evere him is befalle:
Thogh she be the fouleste of alle,
Yet to thonour of wommanhiede
Him thoghte he sholde taken hiede;
So that for pure gentilesse, *good breeding*
As he hire couthe best adresce, *arrange*
In ragges, as she was totore, *tattered*
He set hire on his hors tofore (822)
And forth he takth his weye softe;
No wonder thogh he siketh ofte. *sighs*
Bot as an oule fleth be nihte
Out of alle othre briddes sihte,
Riht so this kniht on dayes brode *in broad daylight*
In clos him hield, and shop his rode *hiding; rode*
On nihtes time, til the tide

That he cam there he wolde abide;   (830)
And prively withoute noise
He bringth this foule grete coise   hag
To his castell in such a wise
That noman mihte hire shappe avise,
Til she into the chambre cam:
Wher he his prive conseil nam
Of suche men as he most troste,
And tolde hem that he nedes moste
This beste wedde to his wif,   beast
For elles hadde he lost his lif.   (840)
  The prive wommen were asent,   trusted; sent for
That sholden ben of his assent:
Hire ragges they anon of drawe,
And, as it was that time lawe,
She hadde bath, she hadde reste,
And was arrayed to the beste.
Bot with no craft of combes brode
They mihte hire hore lockes shode,   separate
And she ne wolde noght be shore   shorn
For no conseil and they therfore,   (850)
With such atir as tho was used,
Ordeinen that it was excused,
And hid so crafteliche aboute,
That noman mihte sen hem oute.   sticking out
Bot when she was fulliche arrayed
And hire atir was al assayed,   inspected
Tho was she foulere on to se:
Bot yit it may non other be,
They were wedded in the niht;
So wo begon was nevere kniht   (860)
As he was thanne of mariage.
And she began to pleye and rage,   sport
As who seith, I am wel inowh;   enough

50

Bot he therof nothing ne lowh,   laughed
For she tok thanne chiere on honde
And clepeth him hire housebonde,
And seith, 'My lord, go we to bedde,
For I to that entente wedde,
That thou shalt be my worldes blisse:'
And profreth him with that to kisse,   (870)
As she a lusty lady were.   willing
His body mihte wel be there,
Bot as of thoght and of memoire
His herte was in purgatoire.
Bot yit for strengthe of matrimoine
He mihte make non essoine,   excuse
That he ne mot algates plye   comply
To gon to bedde of compaignye:
And whan they were abedde naked,
Withoute slep he was awaked;   (880)
He torneth on that other side,
For that he wolde hise yhen hide
Fro lokinge on that foule wiht.
The chambre was al full of liht,
The courtins were of cendal thinne,   silk
This newe brid which lay withinne,   bride
Thogh it be noght with his acord,
In armes she beclipte hire lord,
And preide, as he was torned fro,
He wolde him torne ayeinward tho;   (890)
'For now,' she seith, 'we ben bothe on.'
And he lay stille as eny ston,
Bot evere in on she spak and preide,
And bad him thenke on that he seide,
Whan that he tok hire be the hond.
 He herde and understod the bond,
How he was set to his penance,

And as it were a man in trance
He torneth him al sodeinly,
And sih a lady lay him by   (900)
Of eihtetiene winter age,
Which was the faireste of visage
That evere in al this world he sih:
And as he wolde have take hire nih,
She put hire hand and be his leve
Besoghte him that he wolde leve,
And seith that forto winne or lese
He mot on of tuo thinges chese,
Wher he wol have hire such on niht,
Or elles upon dayes liht,   (910)
For he shal noght have bothe tuo.
And he began to sorwe tho,
In many a wise and caste his thoght,
Bot for al that yit cowthe he noght
Devise himself which was the beste.
And she, that wolde his hertes reste,   ease
Preith that he sholde chese algate,
Til ate last longe and late
He seide: 'O ye, my lives hele,   (919)
Sey what you list in my querele,   case
I not what ansuere I shal yive:
Bot evere whil that I may live,
I wol that ye be my maistresse,
For I can noght myselve gesse
Which is the beste unto my chois.
Thus grante I yow myn hole vois,
Ches for ous bothen, I you preye;
And what as evere that ye seye,
Riht as ye wole so wol I.'

   'My lord,' she seide, 'grant mercy,   (930)
For of this word that ye now sein,

That ye have mad me soverein,
My destine is overpassed,   transcended
That nevere hierafter shal be lassed
My beaute, which that I now have,
Til I be take into my grave;
Bot niht and day as I am now
I shal alwey be such to yow.
The kinges dowhter of Cizile   Sicily
I am, and fell bot sithe awhile,   (940)
As I was with my fader late,   lately
That my stepmoder for an hate,
Which toward me she hath begonne,
Forshop me, til I hadde wonne   transformed
The love and sovereinete
Of what kniht that in his degre
Alle othre passeth of good name:
And, as men sein, ye ben the same,
The ded proeveth it is so;
Thus am I youres evermo.'   (950)
Tho was plesance and joye inowh,
Echon with other pleide and lowh;
They live longe and wel they ferde,
And clerkes that this chance herde
They writen it in evidence,
To teche how that obedience
May wel fortune a man to love
And sette him in his lust above,
As it befell unto this kniht.
    Forthy, my sone, if thou do riht,   (960)
Thou shalt unto thy love obeye,
And folwe hir will be alle weye.

A: Myn holy fader, so I wile:
For ye have told me such a skile

Of this ensample now tofore,
That I shal evermo therfore
Hierafterward myn observance
To Love and to his obeissance
The betre kepe:

*   *   *

BOOK THREE

Confessor:

My sone, a man to beye him pes   buy
Behoveth soffre as Socrates
Ensample lefte, which is write:
And for thou shalt the sothe wite,
Of this ensample what I mene,
Althogh it be now litel sene
Among the men thilke evidence,
Yit he was upon pacience
So sett, that he himself assaye   testing
In thing which mihte him most mispaye   displease
Desireth, and a wickid wif   (11)
He weddeth, which is sorwe and strif
Ayein his ese was contraire.
Bot he spak evere softe and faire,
Til it befell, as it is told,
In winter, whan the day is cold,
This wif was fro the welle come,
Wher that a pot with water nome   filled
She hath, and broghte it into house,   (19)
And sih how that hire sely spouse   simple
Was sett and loked on a bok
Nih to the fir, as he which tok
His ese for a man of age.
And she began the wode rage,
And axeth him what devel he thoghte,
And bar on hond that him ne roghte   asserted
What labour that she toke on honde,
And seith that such an housebonde
Was to a wif noght worth a stre.   straw
He seide nowther nay ne ye,   (30)
Bot hield him stille and let hire chide;

And she, which may hirself noght hide,
Began withinne forto swelle,
And that she broghte in fro the welle,
The waterpot she hente alofte   raised
And bad him speke, and he al softe
Sat stille and noght a word ansuerde;
And she was wroth that he so ferde,
And axeth him if he be ded;
And al the water on his hed   (40)
She pourede oute and bad awake.
Bot he, which wolde noght forsake
His pacience, thanne spak,
And seide how that he fond no lak
In nothing which she hadde do:
For it was winter time tho,
And winter, as be weye of kinde
Which stormy is, as men it finde,
Ferst makth the windes forto blowe,   (49)
And after that withinne a throw   short time
He reineth and the watergates
Undoth; 'and thus my wif algates,   assuredly
Which is with reson wel besein,   equipped
Hath made me bothe wind and rein
After the sesoun of the yer.'
And thanne he sette him nerr the fer,
And as he mihte hise clothes dreide,
That he nomore o word ne seide;
Wherof he gat him somdel reste,
For that him thoghte was the beste.   (60)
    I not if thilke ensample yit
Acordeth with a mannes wit,
To soffre as Socrates tho dede:
And if it falle in eny stede   situation
A man to lese so his galle,   courage

Him oghte among the wommen alle
In Loves court be juggement
The name bere of pacient,
To yive ensample to the goode
Of pacience how that it stode, (70)
That othre men it mihte knowe.
And, sone, if thou at eny throwe
Be tempted ayein pacience,
Tak hiede upon this evidence;
It shal per cas the lasse grieve.

Amans:
My fader, so as I believe,
Of that shal be no maner nede,
For I wol take so good hiede,
That er I falle in such assay,
I thenke eshuie it, if I may. (80)
Bot if ther be oght elles more
Wherof I mihte take lore,
I preye you, so as I dar,
Now telleth, that I may be war,
Som other tale in this matiere.

C: Sone, it is evere good to lere,
Wherof thou miht thy word restreigne,
Er that thou falle in eny peine.
For who that can no conseil hide,
He may noght faile of wo beside, (90)
Which shal befalle er he it wite,
As I finde in the bokes write.

   Yit cam ther nevere good of strif,
To seche in all a mannes lif:
Thogh it beginne on pure game,

Fulofte it torneth into grame   trouble
And doth grevance upon som side.
Wherof the grete clerk Ovide
After the lawe which was tho
Of Jupiter and of Juno   (100)
Makth in his bokes mencioun
How they felle at dissencioun
In manere as it were a borde,   jest
As they begunne forto worde
Among hemself in privete:
And that was upon this degree,
Which of the tuo more amorous is,
Or man or wif. And upon this
They mihten noght acorde in on,
And toke a jugge therupon,   (110)
Which cleped is Tiresias,
And bede him demen in the cas;
And he withoute avisement   consideration
Ayein Juno yaf juggement.
This goddesse upon his ansuere
Was wroth and wolde noght forbere,
Bot tok awey for everemo
The liht fro bothe hise yhen tuo.
Whan Jupiter this harm hath sein,   (119)
An other bienfait therayein   benefit
He yaf, and such a grace him doth,   conferred
That for he wiste he seide soth,
A sothseyere he was for evere:
Bot yit that other were levere,   would rather
Have had the lokinge of his yhe,
Than of his word the prophecye;
Bot how so that the sothe wente,   truth
Strif was the cause of that he hente   suffered
So gret a peine bodily.

My sone, be thou war ther by,   (130)
And hold thy tunge stille clos:
For who that hath his word desclos
Er that he wite what he mene,   knows
He is fulofte nih his tene   sorrow
And lest ful many time grace,   loses
Wher that he wolde his thonk pourchace
And over this, my sone diere,
Of othre men, if thou miht hiere
In privete what they have wroght,
Hold conseil and descoevere it noght,   (140)
For Cheste can no conseil hele,   contentious words
Or be it wo or be it wele:

*   *   *

My sone, thou shalt understonde
That yit towardes Wraththe stonde
Of dedly vices othre tuo:
And forto telle here names so,
It is Contek and Homicide,   dissension
That ben to drede on every side.
Contek, so as the bokes sein,   (149)
Folhast hath to his chamberlein,   rash haste
Be whos conseil al unavised
Is Pacience most despised,
Til Homicide with hem meete.
Fro mercy they ben al unmeete,   far apart
And thus ben they the worste of alle
Of hem whiche unto wrathe falle,
In dede bothe and ek in thoght:
For they acompte here wrathe at noght,
Bot if ther be shedinge of blod;

And thus lich to a beste wod   wild
They knowe noght the God of lif.   (161)
Be so they have or swerd or knif
Here dedly wrathe forto wreke,
Of Pite list hem noght to speke;
No other reson they ne fonge,   take
Bot that they ben of mihtes stronge.
Bot war hem wel in other place,
Where every man behoveth grace,
Bot ther I trowe it shal hem faile,
To whom no mercy mihte availe,   (170)
Bot wroghten upon tiraundye,
That no pite ne mihte hem plye.   bend
Now tell, my sone.

A: Fader, what?

C: If thou hast be coupable of that.

A: My fader, nay, Crist me forbiede:
I speke onliche as of the dede,
Of which I nevere was coupable
Withoute cause resonable.
    Bot this is noght to my matiere   (180)
Of shrifte, why we sitten hiere;
For we ben sett to shrive of Love,
As we begunne ferst above:
And natheles I am beknowe
That as touchende of loves throwe,   pangs
Whan I my wittes overwende,   overturn
Myn hertes contek hath non ende,
Bot evere it stant upon debat
To gret desese of myn astat
As for the time that it lasteth.   (190)

For whan my fortune overcasteth
Hire whiel and is to me so strange,
And that I se she wol noght change,
Than caste I al the world aboute,
And thenke hou I at home and oute
Have al my time in vein despended,
And se noght how to ben amended,
Bot rathere forto be empeired,   made worse
As he that is welnih despeired:
For I ne may no thonk deserve,   (200)
And evere I love and evere I serve,
And evere I am aliche nerr.   equally
Thus, for I stonde in such a wer,   difficulty
I am, as who seith, out of herre,   order
And thus upon myself the werre
I bringe, and putte out alle pes,
That I fulofte in such a res   battle
Am wery of myn oghne lif.
So that of Contek and of strif
I am beknowe and have ansuerd,   (210)
As ye, my fader, now have herd.
Myn herte is wonderly begon   beset
With conseil, wherof Witt is on,   intelligence
Which hath Resoun in compaignye;
Ayein the whiche stant partye
Will, which hath hope of his acord,   desire
And thus they bringen up descord.
Witt and Resoun conseilen ofte
That I myn herte sholde softe,
And that I sholde Will remue   (220)
And put him out of retenue,
Or elles holde him under fote:
For as they sein, if that he mote
His oghne rewle have upon honde,

Ther shal no Witt ben understonde.
Of Hope also they tellen this,
That overal, wher that he is,
He set the herte in jeupartye   at risk
With wishinge and with fantasye,
And is noght trewe of that he seith,   (230)
So that in him ther is no feith:
Thus with Reson and Wit avised
Is Will and Hope alday despised.
Reson seith that I sholde leve
To love, wher ther is no leve
To spede, and Will seith therayein
That such an herte is to vilein,   cowardly
Which dar noght love, and til he spede,
Let Hope serve at such a nede:
He seith ek, where an herte sit   (240)
Al hol governed upon Wit,
He hath this lives lust forlore.
And thus myn herte is al totore
Of such a contek as they make:
Bot yit I may noght Will forsake,
That he nis maister of my thoght,
Or that I spede, or spede noght.

C: Thou dost, my sone, ayein the riht;
Bot Love is of so gret a miht,
His lawe may noman refuse,   (250)
So miht thou thee the betre excuse.
And natheles thou shalt be lerned
That Will sholde evere be governed
Of Reson more than of Kinde.   Instinct

*   *   *

I rede a tale, and telleth this:
The cite which Semiramis
Enclosed hath with wall aboute,
Of worthy folk with many a route
Was enhabited here and there;
Among the whiche tuo ther were   (260)
Above alle othre noble and grete,
Dwellende tho withinne a strete
So nih togedre, as it was sene,
That ther was nothing hem betwene,
Bot wow to wow and wall to wall.   *partition*
This o lord hadde in special
A sone, a lusty bacheler,
In al the toun was no his pier:
In al the toun was non his pier:
That other hadde a dowhter eke,   (270)
Men wisten non so faire as she.   *knew*
And fell so, as it sholde be,
This faire dowhter nih this sone
As they togedre thanne wone,   *dwelt*
Cupide hath so the thinges shape,
They they ne mihte his hand ascape,
That he his fir on hem ne caste:
Wherof her herte he overcaste
To folwe thilke lore and suie   *conform to*
Which nevere man yit miht eshuie;   (280)
And that was Love, as it is happed,
Which hath here hertes so betrapped,
That they be alle weyes seche
How that they mihten winne a speche,
Here wofull peine for to lisse.   *relieve*
    Who loveth wel, it may noght misse,
And namely whan ther be tuo
Of on acord, how so it go,

Bot if that they som weye finde;
For Love is evere of such a kinde (290)
And hath his folk so wel affaited, governed
That howso that it be awaited,
Ther may noman the pourpos lette: hinder
And thus betwen hem tuo they sette
An hole upon a wall to make,
Thurgh which they have her conseil take
At alle times, whan they mihte.
This faire maiden Tisbee hihte,
And he whom that she loveth hote
Was Piramus be name hote. (300)
So longe here lecoun they recorden. knowledge
Til ate laste they acorden
Be nihtes time forto wende
Al one out from the tounes ende,
Wher was a welle under a tree;
And who cam ferst, or she or he,
He sholde stille there abode.
So it befell the nihtes tide
This maiden, which desguised was, (309)
Al prively the softe pas with quiet step
Goth thurgh the large toun unknowe,
Til that she cam withinne a throwe short time
Wher that she liketh forto duelle,
At thilke unhappy freishe welle, ill-fated
Which was also the forest nih.
Wher she comende a leoun sih
Into the feld to take his preye,
In haste and she tho fledde aweye,
So as fortune sholde falle,
For feere and let hire wimpel falle (320)
Nih to the welle upon therbage. the grass
This leoun in his wilde rage

64

A beste, which that he fond oute,
Hath slain, and with his blody snoute,
Whan he hath eten what he wolde,
To drinke of thilke stremes colde
Cam to the welle, where he fond
The wimpel, which out of hire hond
Was falle, and he it hath todrawe,   torn apart
Bebled aboute and al forgnawe;   bloodstained
And thanne he strawhte him forto drinke   went
 Upon the freishe welles brinke,   (332)
And after that out of the plein
He torncth to the wode ayein.
And Tisbee dorste noght remue,
Bot as a bridd which were in mue   cage
Withinne a buish she kepte hire clos
So stille that she noght aros;
Unto hirself and pleigneth ay.
    And fell, whil that she there lay,   (340)
This Piramus cam after sone
Unto the welle, and be the mone
He fond hire wimpel blody there.
Cam nevere yit to mannes ere
Tidinge, ne to mannes sihte
Merveile, which so sore aflihte   disturbed
A mannes herte, as it tho dede
To him, which in the same stede   place
With many a wofull compleiginge
Began his handes forto wringe,   (350)
As he which demeth sikerly   judges
That she be ded: and sodeinly
His swerd al nakid out he breide
In his folhaste, and thus he seide:
'I am cause of this felonye,
So it is resoun that I die,

As she is ded be cause of me.'
And with that word upon his kne
He fell, and to the goddes alle
Up to the hevene he gan to calle, (360)
And preide, sithen it was so
That he may noght his love as tho
Have in this world, that of her grace
He miht hire have in other place,
For hiere wolde he noght abide,
He seith: bot as it shal betide,
The pomel of his swerd to grounde
He sette, and thurgh his herte a wounde
He made up to the bare hilte:
And in this wise himself he spilte (370)
With his folhaste, and deth he nam;
For she withinne a while cam,
Wher he lay ded upon his knif.
So wofull yit was nevere lif
As Tisbee was, whan she him sih:
She mihte noght o word on hih
Speke oute, for hire herte shette,
That of hir lif no pris she sette,
Bot ded swounende doun she fell.
Til after, whanne it so befell (380)
That she out of hire traunce awok,
With many a wofull pitous lok
Hire yhe alwey among she caste
Upon hir love, and ate laste
She cawhte breth and seide thus:
'O thou which cleped art Venus,
Goddesse of Love, and thou, Cupide,
Which Loves cause hast forto guide,
I wot now wel that ye be blinde,
Of thilke unhapp which I now finde (390)

Only betwen my love and me.
This Piramus, which hiere I se
Bledende, what hath he deserved?
For he youre heste hath kept and served,   commands
And was yong and I bothe also:
Helas, why do ye with ous so?
Ye sette oure herte bothe afire,
And maden ous such thing desire
Wherof that we no skile cowthe;   reason
Bot thus oure freishe lusty yowthe   (400)
Withoute joy is al despended,   wasted
Which thing may never ben amended:
For as of me this wol I seye,
That me is levere forto deie
Than live after this sorghful day.'
And with this word, where as he lay,
Hire love in armes she embraseth,
Hire oghne deth and so pourchaseth
That now she wepte and nou she kiste,
Til ate laste, er she it wiste,   (410)
So gret a sorwe is to hire falle,
Which overgoth hire wittes alle.
As she which mihte it noght asterte,   prevent
The swerdes point ayein hire herte
She sette, and fell doun therupon,
Wherof that she was ded anon:
And thus bothe on o swerd bledende
They weren founde ded liggende.

　　Now thou, my sone, hast herd this tale,   (419)
Bewar that of thin oghne bale   harm
Thou be noght cause in thy folhaste,
And kep that thou thy witt ne waste
Upon thy thoght in aventure,
Wherof thy lives forfeture

May falle: and if thou have so thoght
Er this, tell on and hide it noght.

A: My fader, upon loves side
My conscience I woll noght hide,
How that for love of pure wo
I have ben ofte moeved so,   (430)
That with my wishes if I mihte,
A thousand times, I yow plihte,
I hadde storven in a day;   died
And therof I me shrive may,
Though Love fully me ne slowh,
My will to deie was inowh,
So am I of my will coupable:
And yit is she noght merciable,
Which may me yive lif and hele.
Bot that hir list noght with me dele,   (440)
I wot be whos conseil it is,
And him wolde I long time er this,
And yit I wolde and ever shal,
Slen and destruie in special.
The gold of nine kinges londes
Ne sholde him save fro myn hondes,
In my pouer if that he were;
Bot yit him stant of me no fere
For noght that evere I can manace.   threaten
He is the hindrere of my grace,   (450)
Til he be ded I may noght spede;
So mot I nedes taken hiede
And shape how that he were aweye,
If I therto may finde a weye.

C: My sone, tell me now forthy,
Which is that mortiel enemy
That thou manacest to be ded.

A: My fader, it is such a qwed,   villain
That wher I come, he is tofore,
And doth so, that my cause is lore.   (460)

C: What is his name?

A: It is Daunger,
Which is my lady consailer:
For I was nevere yit so slyh,
To come in eny place nih
Wher as she was be niht or day,
That Danger ne was redy ay,
With whom for speche ne for mede   reward
Yit mihte I nevere of love spede;
For evere this I finde soth,   (470)
Al that my lady seith or doth
To me, Daunger shal make an ende,
And that makth al my world miswende:
And evere I axe his help, bot he
May well be cleped sanz pite;   called; without
For ay the more I to him bowe,
The lasse he wol my tale alowe.
He hath my lady so englued,   ensnared
She wol noght that he be remued;
For evere he hangeth on hire seil,   (480)
And is so prive of conseil,
That evere whanne I have oght bede,   requested
I finde Danger in hire stede
And myn ansuere of him I have;
Bot for no mercy that I crave,
Of mercy nevere a point I hadde.
I finde him ansuere ay so badde,
That werse mihte it nevere be:
And thus betwen Danger and me
Is evere werre til he die.   (490)

69

Bot mihte I ben of such maistrye
That I Danger hadde overcome,
With that were al my joye come.
Thus wolde I wonde for no sinne,   turn aside
Ne yit for al this world to winne;
If that I mihte finde a sleihte,   device
To leye al myn astat in weihte,   balance
I wolde him fro the court dissevere,
So that he come ayeinward nevere.
Therfore I wishe and wolde fain   (500)
That he were in som wise slain;
For while he stant in thilke place,
Ne gete I noght my lady grace.
Thus hate I dedly thilke vice,
And wolde he stode in non office
In place wher my lady is;
For if he do, I wot wel this,
That owther shal he deie or I
Withinne a while; and noght forthy
On my lady fulofte I muse,   (510)
How that she may hirself excuse,
If that I deie in such a plit.
Me thenkth she mihte noght be qwit   acquitted
That she ne were an homicide:
And if it sholde so betide,
As God forbiede it sholde be,
Be double weye it is pite.
For I, which al my will and witt
Have yove and served evere yit,   given
And thanne I sholde in such a wise   (520)
In rewardinge of my servise
Be ded, me thenkth it were a rowthe:
And furthermor, to telle trowthe,
She, that hath ever be wel named,

70

Were worthy thanne to be blamed
And of Reson to ben appeled,   impeached
Whan with o word she mihte have heled
A man, and soffreth him so deie.
Ha, who sawh evere such a weye?
Ha, who sawh evere such destresse?   (530)
Withoute pite gentilesse,   nobility
Withoute mercy wommanhede,
That wol so quite a man his mede,   requite
Which evere hath be to Love trewe.
My goode fader, if ye rewe
Upon my tale, tell me now,
And I wol stinte and herkne yow.   cease

C: My sone, attempre thy corage,   restrain; heart
Fro Wraththe, and let thin herte assuage: (539)
For who so wole him underfonge,   receive
He may his grace abide longe,
Er he of Love be received;
And ek also, bot it be weived,
Ther mihte mochel thing befalle,
That sholde make a man to falle
Fro love, that nevere afterward
Ne durste he loke thiderward.
In harde weyes men gon softe,
And er they climbe avise hem ofte: (549)
Men sen alday that rape reweth;   see; haste
And who so wicked ale breweth,
Fulofte he mot the werse drinke:
Betre is to flete than to sinke;
Betre is upon the bridel chiewe
Thanne if he felle and overthrewe,
The hors and stikede in the mir: mud
To caste water in the fir

71

Betre is than brenne up al the hous:
The man which is malicious
And folhastif, fulofte he falleth,   (560)
And selden is whan Love him calleth.
Forthy betre is to soffre a throwe
Than be to wilde and overthrowe;   overthrown
Suffrance hath evere be the beste
To wissen him that secheth reste: guide
And thus, if thou wolt love and spede,
My sone, soffre, as I the rede.
What may the mous ayein the cat?
And for this cause I axe that,
Who may to Love make a werre,   (570)
That he ne hath himself the werre?   worse of it
Love axeth pes and evere shal,
And who that fihteth most withal
Shal lest conquere of his emprise:
For this they tellen that ben wise,
Wicke is to strive and have the werse;
To hasten is noght worth a kerse;   leaf of cress
Thing that a man may noght achieve,
That may noght wel be don at eve,
It mot abide til the morwe.   (580)
Ne haste noght thin oghne sorwe,
My sone, and tak this in thy witt,
He hath noght lost that wel abitt.   endures
    Ensample that it falleth thus,
Thou miht wel take of Piramus,
 Whan he in haste his swerd outdrowh
And on the point himselve slowh
For love of Tisbee pitously,
For he hire wimpel fond blody
And wende a beste hire hadde slain;   (590)
Wher as him oghte have be riht fain,   joyful

72

For she was there al sauf beside;
Bot for he wolde noght abide,
This meschief fell. Forthy be war,
My sone, as I the warne dar,   thee
Do thou nothing in such a res,   haste
For suffrance is the welle of pes.

*   *   *

BOOK FOUR

Confessor:
Among these othre of Slowthes kinde,
Which alle labour set behinde,
And hateth alle besinesse,
Ther is yit on, which Idelnesse
Is cleped, and is the norrice   called; nurse
In mannes kinde of every vice,
Which secheth eases manifold.
In winter doth he noght for cold,
In somer may he noght for hete;
So whether that he frese or swete,   (10)
Or he be inne, or he be oute,   indoors or outside
He wol ben idel al aboute,
Bot if he pleye oght ate dees,   dice
For who as evere take fees   whoever else
And thenkth worshipe to deserve,
Ther is no lord whom he wol serve,
As forto duelle in his servise,
Bot if it were in such a wise,
Of that he seth per aventure
That be lordshipe and coverture   (20)
He may the more stonde stille,
And use his idelnesse at wille.
For he ne wol no travail take
To ride for his lady sake,
Bot liveth al upon his wishes;
And as a cat wolde ete fishes
Withoute wetinge of his cles,   claws
So wolde he do, bot natheles
He faileth ofte of that he wolde.
    My sone, if thou of such a molde   (30)
Art mad, now tell me plein thy shrifte.

Amans:

Nay, fader, God I yive a yifte,   pledge my word to
That toward Love, as be my wit,
Al idel was I nevere yit,
Ne nevere shal, whil I may go.

C: Now, sone, tell me thanne so,
What hast thou don of besishipe
To Love and to the ladyshipe   honour
Of hire which thy lady is?

A: My fader, evere yit er this   (40)
In every place, in every stede,   situation
What so my lady hath me bede,   commanded
With al myn herte obedient
I have therto be diligent.
And if so is she bidde noght,
What thing that thanne into my thoght
Comth ferst, of that I may suffise.   be satisfied
I bowe and profre my servise,
Somtime in chambre, somtime in halle,
Riht as I se the times falle.   (50)
And whan she goth to hiere masse,
That time shal noght overpasse,
That I naproche hir ladyhede,
In aunter if I may hire lede   on the chance that
Unto the chapelle and ayein.
Thanne is noght al my weye in vein,
Somdiel I may the betre fare,
Whan I, that may noght fiele hir bare,
May lede hire clothed in myn arm:
Bot afterward it doth me harm   (60)
Of pure imaginacioun;
For thanne this collacioun   discourse
I make unto myselven ofte,

75

And seye, 'Ha lord, hou she is softe,
How she is round, hou she is smal!
Now wolde God I hadde hire al
Withoute Danger at my wille!'
And thanne I sike and sitte stille,   sigh
Of that I se my besy thoght
Is torned idel into noght.   (70)
Bot for al that lete I ne may,   can't refrain
Whanne I se time an other day,
That I ne do my besinesse
Unto my lady worthinesse.
For I therto my wit afaite   direct
To se the times and awaite
What is to done and what to leve:
And so, whan time is, be hir leve,
What thing she bit me don, I do,
And wher she bidt me gon, I go,   (80)
And whanne hir list to clepe, I come.   call
Thus hath she fulliche overcome
Myn idelnesse til I sterve,   die
So that I mot hire nedes serve,
For as men sein, nede hath no lawe.
Thus mot I nedly to hire drawe,   of necessity
I serve, I bowe, I loke, I loute,   make obeisance
Myn yhe folweth hire aboute,
What so she wole so wol I,
Whan she wol sitte, I knele by,   (90)
And whan she stant, than wol I stonde:
Bot whan she takth hir werk on honde
Of wevinge or enbrouderye,
Than can I noght bot muse and prye   gaze; peer
Upon hir fingres longe and smale,
And now I thenke, and now I tale,   speak
And now I singe, and now I sike,

76

And thus my contienance I pike.   behaviour; select
And if it falle, as for a time
Hir liketh noght abide bime,   (100)
Bot besien hire on other thinges,
Than make I othre taryinges
To dreche forth the longe day,   while away
For me is loth departe away.
And thanne I am so simple of port,   humble; bearing
That forto feigne som desport
I pleye with hire litel hound
Now on the bedd, now on the ground,
Now with hir briddes in the cage;
For ther is non so litel page,   (110)
Ne yit so simple a chamberere,   chambermaid
That I ne make hem alle chere,
Al for they sholde speke wel: so that
Thus mow ye sen my besy whiel,
That goth noght ideliche aboute.
And if hir list to riden oute
On pelrinage or other stede,   pilgrimage
I come, thogh I be noght bede,
And take hire in myn arm alofte
And sette hire in hire sadel softe,   (120)
And so forth lede hire be the bridel,
For that I wolde noght ben idel.
And if hire list to ride in char,   carriage
And thanne I may therof be war,
Anon I shape me to ride
Riht evene be the chares side;
And as I may, I speke among,   at times
And otherwhile I singe a song,
Which Ovide in his bokes made,
And seide, 'O whiche sorwes glade,   (130)
O which wofull prosperite

Belongeth to the proprete
Of Love, who so wole him serve!
And yit therfro may noman swerve,
That he ne mot his lawe obeye.'
And thus I ride forth my weye,
And am riht besy overal
With herte and with my body al,
As I have said you hier tofore.
My goode fader, tell therfore,   (140)
Of idelnesse if I have gilt.

C. My sone, bot thou telle wilt
Oght elles than I may now hiere,
Thou shalt have no penance hiere.
And natheles a man may se,
How now adayes that ther be
Ful manye of suche hertes slowe,   slothful
That wol noght besien hem to knowe
What thing Love is, til ate laste,
That he with strengthe hem overcaste,   (150)
That malgre hem they mote obeye   despite themselves
And don al idelshipe aweye,
To serve wel and besiliche.
Bot, sone, thou art non of swiche,   such
For Love shal the wel excuse: thee
Bot otherwise, if thou refuse
To love, thou miht so per cas   perhaps
Ben idel, as somtime was
A kinges dowhter unavised,   imprudent
Til that Cupide hire hath chastised: (160)
Wherof thou shalt a tale hiere
Acordant unto this matiere.

Of Armenye, I rede thus,
There was a king, which Herupus
Was hote, and he a lusty maide   pleasant
To dowhter hadde, and as men saide
Hire name was Rosiphelee;
Which tho was of gret renomee,   renown
For she was bothe wis and fair
And sholde ben hire fader hair.   heir
Bot she hadde o defalte of slowthe   (171)
Towardes love, and that was rowthe;   a pity
For so wel cowde noman seye,
Which mihte sette hire in the weye
Of loves occupacion
Thurgh non imaginacion;
That scole wolde she noght knowe.   discipline
And thus she was on of the slowe
As of such hertes besinesse,
Til whanne Venus the goddesse,   (180)
Which Loves court hath forto reule,
Hath broght hire into betre reule,
Forth with Cupide and with his miht:
For they merveille how such a wiht,
Which tho was in hir lusty age,
Desireth nother mariage
Ne yit the love of paramours,
Which evere hath be the comun cours
Amonges hem that lusty were.
So was it shewed after there: (190)
For he that hihe hertes loweth
With firy dartes whiche he throweth,
Cupide, which of Love is godd,
In chastisinge hath mad a rodd
To drive awey hir wantounesse;
So that withinne a while, I gesse,   capriciousness

She hadde on such a chance sporned,   occasion; stumbled
That al hire mod was overtorned,
Which ferst she hadde of slow manere:
For thus it fell, as thou shalt hiere.   (200)
Whan come was the monthe of May,
She wolde walke upon a day,
And that was er the sonne ariste;
Of wommen bot a fewe it wiste,
And forth she wente prively
Unto the park was faste by,
Al softe walkende on the gras,
Til she cam ther the launde was,   glade
Thurgh which ther ran a gret rivere.
It thoghte hir fair, and seide, 'Here   (210)
I wole abide under the shawe':   wood
And bad hire wommen to withdrawe,
And ther she stod al one stille,
To thenke what was in hir wille.
She sih the swote floures springe,
She herde glade foules singe,   birds
She sih the bestes in her kinde,
The buck, the do, the hert, the hinde,
The madle go with the femele;   male
And so began ther a querele   (220)
Betwen love and hir oghne herte,
Fro which she couthe noght asterte.   escape
And as she caste hire yhe aboute,
She sih clad in o suite a route   matching garb
Of ladis, wher they comen ride
Along under the wodes side:
On faire amblende hors they sete,
That were al white, fatte and grete,
And everichon they ride on side.   sidesaddle
The sadles were of such a pride,   (230)

With perle and gold so wel begon,   adorned
So riche sih she nevere non;
In kertles and in copes riche   gowns; cloaks
They weren clothed, alle liche,   alike
Departed evene of whit and blew;   divided equally
With alle lustes that she knew   attractions
They were enbrouded overal.
Here bodies weren long and smal,
The beaute faye upon her face   otherworldly
Non erthly thing it may desface;   may mar it
Corones on here hed they beere,   (241)
As ech of hem a qweene weere,
That al the gold of Cresus halle
The leste coronal of alle
Ne mihte have boght after the worth:
Thus come they ridende forth.
        The kinges dowhter, which this sih,
For pure abaisht drowh hire adrih   surprise; drew back
And hield hire clos under the bowh,
And let hem passen stille inowh;   (250)
For as hire thoghte in hire avis,   opinion
To hem that were of such a pris   excellence
She was noght worthy axen there,
Fro when they come or what they were:
Bot levere than this worldes good   rather
She wolde have wist hou that it stod,
And putte hire hed alitel oute;
And as she lokede hire aboute,
She sih comende under the linde   trees
A womman up an hors behinde.   (260)
The hors on which she rod was blak,
Al lene and galled on the back,   with sores
And haltede, as he were encluyed,   limped; as if; crippled
Wherof the womman was annuyed;   weary

81

Thus was the hors in sory plit,
Bot for al that a sterre whit   star
Amiddes in the front he hadde.
Hir sadel ek was wonder badde,
In which the wofull womman sat,
And natheles ther was with that   (270)
A riche bridel for the nones   occasion
Of gold and preciouse stones.
Hire cote was somdiel totore;   tattered
Aboute hir middel twenty score
Of horse haltres and wel mo   many more
Ther hyngen ate time tho.

 Thus whan she cam the lady nih,
Than tok she betre hiede and sih
This womman fair was of visage,
Freysh, lusty, yong and of tendre age;   (280)
And so this lady, ther she stod,
Bethoghte hire wel and understod
That this, which com ridende tho,
Tidinges couthe telle of tho,
Which as she sih tofore ride,
And putte hir forth and preide abide,
And seide, 'Ha, suster, let me hiere,
What ben they that now riden hiere,
And ben so richeliche arrayed?'

 This womman, which com so esmayed, troubled
Ansuerde with ful softe speche,   (291)
And seith, 'Ma dame, I shal you teche.
These ar of tho that whilom were
Servantz to Love, and trowthe beere, kept faith
Ther as they hadde here herte set.
Fare wel, for I may noght be let: hindered
Ma dame, I go to my servise,
So moste I haste in alle wise;

Forthy, Ma dame, yif me leve,
I may noght longe with you leve.'   remain
  'Ha, goode soster, yit I preye,   (301)
Tell me why ye ben so beseye   dressed
And with these haltres thus begon.'   adorned
  'Ma dame, whilom I was on
That to my fader hadde a king;
Bot I was slow, and for no thing
Me liste noght to Love obeye,
And that I now ful sore abeye.   pay for
For I whilom no love hadde,
Myn hors is now so fieble and badde,   (310)
And al totore is myn aray,
And every yeer this freishe May
These lusty ladis ride aboute,
And I mot nedes suie here route   follow; troop
In this manere as ye now se,
And trusse here haltres forth with me,   carry
And am bot as here horse knave.
Non other office I ne have,
Hem thenkth I am worthy nomore,
For I was slow in loves lore,   (320)
Whan I was able forto lere,
And wolde noght the tales hiere
Of hem that couthen love teche.'
  'Now tell me thanne, I yow beseche,
Wherof that riche bridel serveth.'
  With that hire chere awey she swerveth,   face
And gan to wepe, and thus she tolde:
'This bridel, which ye nou beholde
So riche upon myn horse hed,—
Ma dame, afore, er I was ded,   (330)
Whan I was in my lusty lif,
Ther fel into myn herte a strif

83

Of love, which me overcom,
So that therafter hiede I nom   I took heed
And thoghte I wolde love a kniht:
That laste wel a fourteniht,
For it no lengere mihte laste,
So nih my lif was ate laste.   at its end
Bot now, allas, to late war
That I ne hadde him loved ar: sooner
For deth cam so in haste bime,   (341)
Er I therto hadde eny time,
That it ne mihte ben achieved.
Bot for al that I am relieved,
Of that my will was good therto,
That Love soffreth it be so
That I shal swiche a bridel were.
Now have ye herd al myn ansuere:
To Godd, Ma dame, I you betake,
And warneth alle for my sake,   (350)
Of love that they ben noght idel,
And bidd hem thenke upon my bridel.'
And with that word al sodeinly
She passeth, as it were a sky,   cloud
Al clene out of this lady sihte:
And tho for fiere hire herte afflihte,   was distressed
And seide to hirself, 'Helas!
I am riht in the same cas.
Bot if I live after this day,
I shal amende it, if I may.'   (360)
And thus homward this lady wente;
And changede al hire ferste entente,
Withinne hire herte and gan to swere
That she none haltres wolde bere.

    Lo, sone, hier miht thou taken hiede,
How idelnesse is forto drede,

Namliche of love, as I have write.   particularly
For thou miht understonde and wite,
Among the gentil nacion
Love is an occupacion,   (370)
Which forto kepe hise lustes save   its desires true
Sholde every gentil herte have:
For as the lady was chastised,
Riht so the kniht may ben avised,
Which idel is and wol noght serve
To Love, he may per cas deserve
A grettere peine than she hadde.
Whan she aboute with hire ladde
The horse haltres; and forthy
Good is to be wel war therby.   (380)
Bot forto loke aboven alle,
These maidens, hou so that it falle,
They sholden take ensample of this
Which I have told, for soth it is.
    My lady Venus, whom I serve,
What womman wole hire thonk descrve,
She may noght thilke love eshuie
Of paramours, bot she mot suie
Cupides lawe, and natheles   (389)
Men sen such love sielde in pes,   seldom
That it nis evere upon aspye   observation
Of janglinge and of fals envye
Fulofte medlid with disese: mingled
Bot thilke love is wel at ese,
Which set is upon mariage;
For that dar shewen the visage
In alle places openly,
A gret mervaile it is forthy,
How that a maiden wolde lette,   prevent it
That she hir time ne besette   employ

To haste unto that ilke feste,   (401)
Wherof the love is al honeste.
Men may recovere lost of good,
Bot so wis man yit nevere stod,
Which may recovere time lore:
So may a maiden wel therfore
Ensample take, of that she strangeth
Hir love, and longe er that she changeth
Hir herte upon hir lustes greene
To mariage, as it is seene.   (410)
For thus a yer or tuo or thre
She lest, er that she wedded be,   wastes
Whil she the charge mihte bere
Of children, whiche the world forbere   forego
Ne may, bot if it sholde faile.
Bot what maiden hire esposaile
Wol tarye, whan she take may,
She shal per chance an other day
Be let, whan that hire lievest were.   most willing

*   *   *

A: My fader, as toward the love   (420)
Of maidens forto telle trowthe,
Ye have thilke vice of Slowthe,
Me thenkth, riht wonder wel declared,
That ye the wommen have noght spared
Of hem that tarien so behinde.
Bot yit it falleth in my minde,
Toward the men hou that ye spieke
Of hem that wole no travail sieke
In cause of love upon decerte: as to merit
To speke in wordes so coverte   guarded
I not what travaill that ye mente.   (431)

C: My sone, and after myn entente
I woll thee telle what I thoghte,
Hou whilom men here loves boghte
Thurgh gret travaill in strange londes,
Wher that they wroghten with here hondes
Of armes many a worthy dede,
In sondry place as men may rede.

    That every love of pure kinde
Is ferst forthdrawe, wel I finde: cultivated
Bot natheles yit overthis   (441)
Decerte doth so that it is
The rather had in many place.
Forthy who secheth loves grace,
Wher that these worthy wommen are,
He may noght thanne himselve spare
Upon his travail forto serve,
Wherof that he may thonk deserve,
There as these men of armes be,
Somtime over the grete Se: Mediterranean
So that be londe and ek be shipe   (451)
He mot travaile for worshipe
And make manye hastyf rodes,   speedy; journeys
Somtime in Prus, somtime in Rodes,   Prussia; Rhodes
And somtime into Tartarye;   Tartary
So that these heraldz on him crye,
'Vailant, vailant, lo, wher he goth!'
And thanne he yifth hem gold and cloth,
So that his fame mihte springe,
And to his lady ere bringe   (460)
Som tidinge of his worthinesse;
So that she mihte of his prouesce
Of that she herde men recorde,
The betre unto his love acorde

And Danger pute out of hire mod,   mind
Whanne alle men recorden good,
And that she wot wel, for hir sake
That he no travail wol forsake.
    My sone, of this travail I meene:
Nou shrif thee, for it shal be sene   (470)
If thou art idel in this cas.

_A:_ My fader ye, and evere was:
For as me thenketh trewely
That every man doth mor than I
As of this point, and if so is
That I have oght so don er this,
It is so litel of accompte,
As who seith, it may noght amonte   be sufficient
To winne of Love his lusty yifte.
For this I telle you in shrifte,   (480)
That me were levere hir love winne
Than Kaire and al that is ther inne: Cairo
And forto slen the hethen alle,
I not what good ther mihte falle,
So mochel blod thogh ther be shad.
This finde I writen, hou Crist bad
That noman other sholde sle.
What sholde I winne over the se,
If I my lady loste at hom?
Bot passe they the salte fom,   let those
To whom Crist bad they sholden preche   (491)
To all the world and his feith teche:
Bot now they rucken in here nest   crouch
And resten as hem liketh best
In al the swetnesse of delices.   delights
Thus they defenden ous the vices,
And sitte hemselven al amidde;

To slen and feihten they ous bidde
Hem whom they sholde, as the bok seith,
Converten unto Cristes feith.   (500)
Bot hierof have I gret mervaile,
Hou they wol bidde me travaile:
A Sarazin if I sle shal,
I sle the soule forth withal,
And that was nevere Cristes lore.
Bot nou ho ther, I seye nomore.

    Bot I wol speke upon my shrifte;
And to Cupide I make a yifte,   pledge
That who as evere pris deserve
Of armes, I wol Love serve;   (510)
And thogh I sholde hem bothe kepe,
Als wel yit wolde I take kepe
Whan it were time to abide,
As forto travaile and to ride:
For how as evere a man laboure,
Cupide appointed hath his houre.

    For I have herd it telle also,
Achilles lefte hise armes so
Bothe of himself and of his men
At Troye for Polixenen,   (520)
Upon hire love whanne he fell,
That for no chance that befell
Among the Grecs or up or doun,
He wolde noght ayein the toun
Ben armed, for the love of hire.
And so me thenketh, lieve sire,
A man of armes may him reste
Somtime in hope for the beste,
If he may finde a weye nerr.
What sholde I thanne go so ferr   (530)
In strange londes many a mile

To ride, and lese at hom therwhile
My love? It were a short beyete   possession
To winne chaf and lese whete.
Bot if my lady bidde wolde,
That I for hire love sholde
Travaile, me thenkth trewely
I mihte fle thurghout the sky,
And go thurghout the depe se,
For al ne sette I at a stre   straw
What thonk that I mihte elles gete.   (541)
What helpeth it a man have mete,   food
Wher drinke lacketh on the bord?
What helpeth eny mannes word
To seye hou I travaile faste,
Wher as me faileth ate laste
That thing which I travaile fore?
O in good time were he bore,   born
That mihte atteigne such a mede.   reward
Bot certes if I mihte spede   (550)
With eny maner besinesse
Of worldes travail, thanne I gesse,
Ther sholde me no idelshipe
Departen fro hir ladishipe.
Bot this I se, on dayes nou
The blinde god, I wot noght hou,
Cupido, which of Love is lord,
He set the thinges in discord,
That they that lest to love entende   least
Fulofte he wole hem yive and sende   (560)
Most of his grace; and thus I finde
That he that sholde go behinde,
Goth many a time ferr tofore:
So wot I noght riht wel therfore,
On whether bord that I shal seile.   what course

Thus can I noght myself conseile,
Bot al I sette on aventure,   chance
And am, as who seith, out of cure
For ought that I can seye or do:
For everemore I finde it so,   (570)
The more besinesse I leye,
The more that I knele and preye
With goode wordes and with softe,
The more I am refused ofte,
With besinesse and may noght winne.
And in good feith that is gret sinne;
For I may seye of dede and thoght
That idel man have I be noght;
For hou as evere I be deslayed,   hindered
Yit evermore I have assayed.   (580)
Bot thogh my besinesse laste,
Al is bot idel ate laste,
For whan theffect is idelnesse,
I not what thing is besinesse.
Sey, what availeth al the dede,
Which nothing helpeth ate nede?
For the fortune of every fame
Shal of his ende bere a name.
And thus for oght is yit befalle,
An idel man I wol me calle   (590)
As after myn entendement:
Bot upon youre amendement,
Myn holy fader, as you semeth,
My reson and my cause demeth.

C: My sone, I have herd thy matiere,
Of that thou hast thee shriven hiere:
And forto speke of idel fare,
Me semeth that thou tharst noght care,   ought

Bot only that thou miht noght spede.
And therof, sone, I wol thee rede,   advise
Abid, and haste noght to faste;   (601)
Thy dees ben every day to caste,   dice
Thou nost what chance shal betide.
Betre is to waite upon the tide
Than rowe ayein the stremes stronge:
For thogh so be thee thenketh longe,
Per cas the revolucion
Of heven and thy condicion
Ne be noght yit of on acord.
Bot I dar make this record   (610)
To Venus, whos prest that I am,
That sithen that I hidir cam
To hiere, as she me bad, thy lif,
Wherof thou elles be gultif,
Thou miht hierof thy conscience
Excuse, and of gret diligence,
Which thou to love hast so despended,
Thou oghtest wel to be comended.
Bot if so be that ther oght faile,
Of that thou slowthest to travaile   (620)
In armes forto ben absent,
And for thou makst an argument
Of that thou seidest hiere above,
Hou Achilles thurgh strengthe of love
Hise armes lefte for a throwe,   time
Thou shalt an other tale knowe,
Which is contraire, as thou shalt wite.
For this a man may finde write,
Whan that knihthode shal be werred,
Lust may noght thanne be preferred;   (630)
The bedd mot thanne be forsake
And shield and spere on honde take,

92

Which thing shal make hem after glade,
Whan they ben worthy knihtes made.

*   *   *

Toward the Slowe progenye   *of sloth*
Ther is yit on of compaignye,
And he is cleped Sompnolence,
Which doth to Slouthe his reverence,
As he which is his chamberlein,
That many an hundrid time hath lein   (640)
To slepe, whan he sholde wake.
He hath with Love trewes take,   *truce*
That wake who so wake wile,
If he may couche a doun his bile,
He hath al wowed what him list;
That ofte he goth to bedde unkist,
And seith that for no druerye   *beloved*
He wol noght leve his sluggardye.
For thogh noman it wole allowe,
To slepe levere than to wowe,   *rather*
Is his manere, and thus on nihtes,   (651)
Whan that he seth the lusty knihtes
Revelen, wher these wommen are,
Awey he skulketh as an hare,
And goth to bedde and leith him softe,
And of his slouthe he dremeth ofte
Hou that he stiketh in the mir,   *mire*
And hou he sitteth be the fir
And claweth on his bare shankes,
And hou he climbeth up the bankes   (660)
And falleth into slades depe.   *valleys*
Bot thanne who so toke kepe,

93

Whanne he is falle in such a drem,
Riht as a ship ayein the strem,
He routeth with a slepy noise,   snores
And brustleth as a monkes froise,   sizzles; pancake
Whanne it is throwe into the panne.
And otherwhile sielde whanne   seldom
That he may dreme a lusty swevene,   dream
Him thenkth as thogh he were in hevene   (670)
And as the world were holy his:
And thanne he spekth of that and this,
And makth his exposicion
After the disposicion
Of that he wolde, and in such wise
He doth to Love all his service;
I not what thonk he shal deserve.
Bot, sone, if thou wolt Love serve,
I rede that thou do noght so.

A: Ha, goode fader, certes no.   (680)
I hadde levere be my trowthe,
Er I were set on such a slouthe
And beere such a slepy snoute,
Bothe yhen of myn hed were oute.
For me were betre fully die,
Thanne I of such a slugardye
Hadde eny name, God me shilde;
For whan my moder was with childe,
And I lay in hire wombe clos,
I wolde rathere Atropos,   (690)
Which is goddesse of alle Deth,
Anon as I hadde eny breth,
Me hadde fro my moder cast.
Bot now I am nothing agast,
I thonke Godd; for Lachesis,

Ne Cloto, which hire felawe is,
Me shopen no such destine,
Whan they at my nativite
My weerdes setten as they wolde;   fates
Bot they me shopen that I sholde   (700)
Eshuie of slep the truandise,
So that I hope in such a wise
To Love forto ben excused,
That I no sompnolence have used.
For certes, fader Genius,
Yit into nou it hath be thus,
At alle time if it befelle
So that I mihte come and duelle
In place ther my lady were,
I was noght slow ne slepy there: (710)
For thanne I dar wel undertake,
That whanne hir list on nihtes wake
In chambre as to carole and daunce,
Me thenkth I may me more avaunce,
If I may gon upon hir hond,
Thanne if I wonne a kinges lond.
For whanne I may hire hand beclippe,
With such gladnesse I daunce and skippe,
Me thenkth I touche noght the flor;
The ro, which renneth on the mor,   roe
Is thanne noght so liht as I: (721)
So mow ye witen wel forthy,   may
That for the time slep I hate.
And whanne it falleth othergate,   otherwise
So that hire like noght to daunce,
Bot on the dees to caste chaunce   tell fortunes
Or axe of love som demande,
Or elles that hir list comaunde
To rede and here of Troilus,

Riht as she wole or so or thus,   (730)
I am al redy to consente.
And if so is that I may hente   seize
Somtime among a good leisir,   opportunity
So as I dar of my desir
I telle a part; bot whanne I preye,
Anon she bidt me go my weye
And seith it is ferr in the niht;
And I swere it is even liht:
Bot as it falleth ate laste,
Ther may no worldes joye laste,   (740)
So mot I nedes fro hire wende
And of my wache make an ende:
And if she thanne hiede toke,
Hou pitousliche on hire I loke,
Whan that I shal my leve take,
Hire oghte of mercy forto slake
Hire Daunger, which seith evere nay.
    Bot he seith often, 'Have good day,'
That loth is forto take his leve:
Therfore, while I may beleve,   (750)
I tarye forth the niht along,   linger
For it is noght on me along   not my fault
To slep that I so sone go,
Til that I mot algate so;
And thanne I bidde Godd hire se,   protect
And so doun knelende on my kne
I take leve, and if I shal,
I kisse hire, and go forth withal.
And otherwhile, if that I dore,
Er I come fully to the dore,   (760)
I torne ayein and feigne a thing,
As thogh I hadde lost a ring
Or somwhat elles, for I wolde

Kisse hire eftsones, if I sholde,   again
Bot selden is that I so spede.
And whanne I se that I mot nede
Departen, I departe, and thanne
With al myn herte I curse and banne   condemn
That evere slep was mad for yhe;
For, as me thenkth, I mihte dryhe   endure
Withoute slep to waken evere,   (771)
So that I sholde noght dissevere   be separated
Fro hire, in whom is al my liht:
And thanne I curse also the niht
With al the will of my corage,
And seye, 'Awey, thou blake image,
Which of thy derke cloudy face
Makst al the worldes liht deface,
And causest unto slep a weye,
Be which I mot nou gon aweye   (780)
Out of my lady compaignye.
O slepy niht, I thee defye,
And wolde that thou leye in presse   down below
With Proserpine the goddesse
And with Pluto the helle king:
For til I se the dayes spring,
I sette slep noght at a rishe.'   rush
And with that word I sike and wishe,
And seye, 'Ha, why ne were it day?
For yit my lady thanne I may   (790)
Beholde, thogh I do nomore.'
And efte I thenke forthermore,   then
To som man hou the niht doth ese,
Whan he hath thing that may him plese
The longe nihtes be his side,
Where as I faile and go beside.   am slighted
Bot slep, I not wherof it serveth,

Of which noman his thonk deserveth
To gete him love in eny place,
Bot is an hindrere of his grace   (800)
And makth him ded as for a throwe,   time
Riht as a stok were overthrowe.   dead log
And so, my fader, in this wise
The slepy nihtes I despise,
And evere amiddes of my tale
I thenke upon the nihtingale,
Which slepeth noght be weye of kinde
For love, in bokes as I finde.
Thus ate laste I go to bedde,
And yit min herte lith to wedde   lies in pawn
With hire, where as I cam fro;   (811)
Thogh I departe, he wol noght so,
Ther is no lock may shette him oute,
Him nedeth noght to gon aboute,
That perce may the harde wall;
Thus is he with hire overall,
That be hire lief, or be hire loth,
Into hire bedd myn herte goth,
And softly takth hire in his arm
And fieleth hou that she is warm,   (820)
And wisheth that his body were
To fiele that he fieleth there.
And thus myselven I tormente,
Til that the dede slep me hente:
Bot thanne be a thousand score
Welmore than I was tofore
I am tormented in my slep,
Bot that I dreme is noght of shep;
For I ne thenke noght on wulle,   (829)
Bot I am drecched to the fulle   tormented
Of love, that I have to kepe,   in my keeping

98

That nou I lawhe and nou I wepe,
And nou I lese and nou I winne,
And nou I ende and nou beginne.
And otherwhile I dreme and mete   dream
That I al one with hire mete
And that Danger is left behinde;
And thanne in slep such joye I finde,
That I ne bede nevere awake.   beg
Bot after, whanne I hiede take,   (840)
And shal arise upon the morwe,
Thanne is al torned into sorwe,
Noght for the cause I shal arise,
Bot for I mette in such a wise,
And ate laste I am bethoght
That al is vein and helpeth noght:
Bot yit me thenketh be my wille   had I my wish
I wolde have leye and slepe stille,
To meten evere of such a swevene,   dream
For thanne I hadde a slepy hevene.   (850)

C: My sone, and for thou tellest so,
A man may finde of time ago
That many a swevene hath be certein,   true
Al be it so, that som men sein
That swevenes ben of no credence.
Bot forto shewe in evidence
That they fulofte sothe thinges
Betokne, I thenke in my writinges
To telle a tale therupon,
Which fell be olde dayes gon.   (860)

   This finde I write in poesye:
Ceix the king of Trocinye
Hadde Alceone to his wif,

99

Which as hire oghne hertes lif
Him loveth; and he hadde also
A brother, which was cleped tho
Dedalion, and he per cas   *by chance*
Fro kinde of man forshape was   *transformed*
Into a goshauk of liknesse;
Wherof the king gret hevinesse   (870)
Hath take, and thoghte in his corage
To gon upon a pelrinage   *pilgrimage*
Into a strange regioun,
Wher he hath his devocioun
To don his sacrifice and preye,
If that he mihte in eny weye
Toward the goddes finde grace   *from*
His brother hele to pourchace,
So that he mihte be reformed
Of that he hadde be transformed.   (880)
To this pourpos and to this ende
This king is redy forto wende,
As he which wolde go be shipe;
And forto don him felashipe
His wif unto the see him broghte,
With al hire herte and him besoghte,
That he the time hire wolde sein,
Whan that he thoghte come ayein:
'Withinne,' he seith, 'tuo monthe day.'
And thus in al the haste he may   (890)
He tok his leve, and forth he seileth
Wepende, and she hirself beweileth,
And torneth hom, ther she cam fro.
Bot whan the monthes were ago,
The whiche he sette of his cominge,
And that she herde no tidinge,
Ther was no care forto seche:

Wherof the goddes to beseche
Tho she began in many wise,
And to Juno hire sacrifise　　　　　　　　　　　　(900)
Above alle othre most she dede,
And for hir lord she hath so bede
To wite and knowe hou that he ferde,
That Juno the goddesse hire herde,
Anon and upon this matiere
She bad Iris hir messagere
To Slepes hous that she shal wende,
And bidde him that he make an ende
Be swevene and shewen al the cas
Unto this lady, hou it was.　　　　　　　　　　　(910)
　　This Iris, fro the hihe stage　　　　　　　　place
Which undertake hath the message,
Hire reiny cope dede upon,　　　　　　　cloak; put on
The which was wonderly begon　　　　　　　adorned
With colours of diverse hewe,
An hundred mo than men it knewe；
The hevene lich unto a bowe
She bende, and so she cam doun lowe,
The god of Slep wher that she fond.
And that was in a strange lond,　　　　　　　(920)
Which marcheth upon Chimerie：
For ther, as seith the poesye,
The god of Slep hath mad his hous,
Which of entaille is merveilous.　　　　　　　design
Under an hell ther is a cave,　　　　　　　hill
Which of the sonne may noght have,
So that noman may knowe ariht
The point betwen the day and niht：
Ther is no fir, ther is no sparke,
Ther is no dore, which may charke,　　　　　creak
Wherof an yhe sholde unshette,　　　　　　　(931)

101

So that inward ther is no lette.   hindrance
And forto speke of that withoute,
Ther stant no gret tree nih aboute
Wher on ther mihte crowe or pie
Alihte, forto clepe or crye:
Ther is no cok to crowe day,
Ne beste non which noise may
The hell, bot al aboute round
Ther is growende upon the ground   (940)
Popy, which berth the sed of slep,
With othre herbes suche an hep.   a host of
A stille water for the nones   quiet stream
Rennende upon the smale stones,
Which hihte of Lethes the rivere,
Under that hell in such manere
Ther is, which yifth gret appetit
To slepe. And thus full of delit
Slep hath his hous; and of his couche   (949)
Withinne his chambre if I shal touche   touch on
Of hebenus that slepy tree   ebony
The bordes al aboute be,
And for he sholde slepe softe,
Upon a fethrebed alofte
He lith with many a pilwe of doun: pillow
The chambre is strowed up and doun
With swevenes many thousendfold.
Thus cam Iris into this hold,   abode
And to the bedd, which is al blak,
She goth, and ther with Slep she spak,   (960)
And in the wise as she was bede
The message of Juno she dede.
Fulofte hir wordes she reherceth,   repeats
Er she his slepy eres perceth;
With mochel wo bot ate laste

102

His slombrende yhen he upcaste
And seide hir that it shal be do.
Wherof among a thousend tho,
Withinne his hous that slepy were,
In special he ches out there   (970)
Thre, whiche sholden do this dede:
The ferste of hem, so as I rede,
Was Morpheus, the whos nature
Is forto take the figure
Of what persone that him liketh,
Wherof that he fulofte entriketh
The lif which slepe shal be nihte;   person
And Ithecus that other hihte,
Which hath the vois of every soun,   can reproduce
The chiere and the condicioun   expression; quality
Of every lif, what so it is: (981)
The thridde suiende after this   following
Is Panthasas, which may transforme
Of every thing the rihte forme,
And change it in an other kinde.
Upon hem thre, so as I finde,
Of swevenes stant al thapparence,
Which otherwhile is evidence   sometimes
And otherwhile bot a jape.
Bot natheles it is so shape,   (990)
That Morpheus be niht al one
Appiereth until Alceone
In liknesse of hir housebonde
Al naked ded upon the stronde,
And hou he dreinte in special   specifically
These othre tuo it shewen al.
The tempeste of the blake cloude,
The wode see, the windes loude,   raging
Al this she mette, and sih him dien;

103

Wherof that she began to crien, (1000)
Slepende abedde ther she lay,
And with that noise of hire affray   *outcry*
Hir wommen sterten up aboute,
Whiche of here lady were in doute   *fearful for*
And axen hire hou that she ferde;
And she, riht as she sih and herde,
Hir swevene hath told hem everydel.
And they it halsen alle wel   *interpret*
And sein it is a tokne of goode;
Bot til she wiste hou that it stode,   (1010)
She hath no confort in hire herte,
Upon the morwe and up she sterte,
And to the see, wher that she mette
The body lay, withoute lette
She drowh, and whan that she cam nih,   *went*
Stark ded, hise armes sprad, she sih
Hire lord flietende upon the wawe.   *floating*
Wherof hire wittes ben withdrawe,
And she, which tok of deth no kepe,
Anon forth lepte into the depe   (1020)
And wolde have cawht him in hire arm.

    This infortune of double harm   *misfortune*
The goddes fro the hevene above
Behielde, and for the trowthe of love,
Which in this worthy lady stod,
They have upon the salte flod
Hire dreinte lord and hire also
Fro deth to live torned so,
That they ben shapen into briddes
Swimmende upon the wawe amiddes.   (1030)
And whan she sih hire lord livende
In liknesse of a bridd swimmende,
And she was of the same sort,

So as she mihte do desport,
Upon the joye which she hadde
Hire winges bothe abrod she spradde,
And him, so as she may suffise,
Beclipte and keste in such a wise,
As she was whilom wont to do: once
Hire winges for hire armes tuo   (1040)
She tok, and for hire lippes softe
Hire harde bile, and so fulofte
She fondeth in hire briddes forme,   endeavours
If that she mihte hirself conforme
To do the plesance of a wif,
As she dede in that other lif:
For thogh she hadde hir pouer lore,   power; lost
Hir will stod as it was tofore,
And serveth him so as she may.
Wherof into this ilke day   (1050)
Togedre upon the see they wone,   dwell
Wher many a dowhter and a sone
They bringen forth of briddes kinde;
And for men sholden take in minde
This Alceoun the trewe queene,
Hire briddes yit, as it is seene,
Of Alceoun the name bere.
    Lo thus, my sone, it may thee stere
Of swevenes forto take kepe,
For ofte time a man aslepe   (1060)
May se what after shal betide.
Forthy it helpeth at som tide
A man to slepe, as it belongeth,
Bot Slowthe no lif underfongeth   accepts
Which is to love appourtenant.   appropriate

A: My fader, upon covenant
I dar wel make this avou,
Of all my lif that into nou,
Als fer as I can understonde,
Yit tok I nevere slep on honde,   (1070)
Whan it was time forto wake;
For thogh myn yhe it wolde take,
Myn herte is evere therayein.   opposed to that
Bot natheless to speke it plein,
Al this that I have seid you hiere
Of my wakinge, as ye may hiere,
It toucheth to my lady swete;
For otherwise, I you behiete,   promise
In strange place whanne I go,
Me list nothing to wake so.   (1080)
For whan the wommen listen pleye,   wish to
And I hir se noght in the weye,   as I go about
Of whom I sholde merthe take,
Me list noght longe forto wake,
Bot if it be for pure shame,
Of that I wolde eshuie a name,   avoid
That they ne sholde have cause non
To seye, 'Ha, lo, wher goth such on,
That hath forlore his contenaunce!'   lost
And thus among I singe and daunce,   (1090)
And feigne lust ther as non is.
For ofte sithe I fiele this;
Of thoght, which in my herte falleth
Whanne it is niht, myn hed appalleth, makes anxious
And that is for I se hire noght,
Which is the wakere of my thoght: stirrer up
And thus as timliche as I may,   soon
Fulofte whanne it is brod day,
I take of all these othre leve

And go my weye and they beleve,   (1100)
That sen per cas here loves there;
And I go forth as noght ne were
Unto my bedd, so that al one
I may ther ligge and sighe and grone
And wishen al the longe niht,
Til that I se the dayes liht.
I not if that be sompnolence,
Bot upon youre conscience,
Myn holy fader, demeth ye.   judge

C: My sone, I am wel paid with thee,   pleased
Of slep that thou the sluggardye   (111)
Be nihte in loves compaignye
Eshuied hast, and do thy peine
So that thy love thar noght pleine: complain
For Love upon his lust wakende   desire
Is evere, and wolde that non ende
Were of the longe nihtes set.
Wherof that thou be war the bet,
To telle a tale I am bethoght,
Hou love and slep acorden noght.   (1120)

   For love who that list to wake
By nihte, he may ensample take
Of Cephalus, whan that he lay
With Aurora that swete may   maiden
In armes all the longe niht.
Bot whanne it drogh toward the liht,
That he withinne his herte sih
The day which was amorwe nih,
Anon unto the sonne he preide
For lust of love, and thus he seide: (1130)
   'O Phebus, which the dayes liht

107

Governest, til that it be niht,
And gladest every creature
After the lawe of thy nature,—
Bot natheles ther is a thing,
Which only to the knouleching
Belongeth as in privete   secrecy
To Love and to his duete,
Which asketh noght to ben apert,   overt
Bot in cilence and in covert   secrecy
Desireth forto be beshaded: (1141)
And thus whan that thy liht is faded
And Vesper sheweth him alofte,
And that the niht is long and softe,
Under the cloudes derke and stille
Thanne hath this thing most of his wille.
Forthy unto thy mihtes hihe,
As thou which art the dayes yhe,
Of Love and miht no conseil hide,
Upon this derke nihtes tide   (1150)
With al myn herte I thee beseeche
That I plesance mihte seche
With hire which lith in min armes.
Withdrawh the banere of thin armes,
And let thy lihtes ben unborn,
And in the signe of Capricorn,
The hous appropred to Satorne,
I preye that thou wolt sojorne,
Wher ben the nihtes derke and longe:
For I my love have underfonge,   (1160)
Which lith hier be my side naked,
As she which wolde ben awaked,
And me lest nothing forto slepe.
So were it good to take kepe
Nou at this nede of my preyere,

And that the like forto stiere
Thy firy darte, and so ordeigne,
That thou thy swifte hors restreigne
Lowe under erthe in Occident,   *the West*
That they towardes Orient   (1170)
Be cercle go the longe weye.
    And ek to thee, Diane, I preye,
Which cleped art of thy noblesse
The nihtes mone and the goddesse,
That thou to me be gracious:
And in Cancro thin oghne hous
Ayein Phebus in opposit
Stond al this time, and of delit   *delightedly*
Behold Venus with a glad yhe.
For thanne upon astronomye   (1180)
Of due constellacion
Thou makst prolificacion,
And dost that children ben begete:
Which grace if that I mihte gete,
With al myn herte I wolde serve
Be nihte, and thy vigile observe.'
    Lo, thus this lusty Cephalus
Preide unto Phebe and to Phebus
The niht in lengthe forto drawe,
So that he mihte do the lawe   (1190)
In thilke point of Loves heste,   *commandment*
Which cleped is the nihtes feste,   *feast*
Withoute slep of sluggardye;
Which Venus out of compaignye   *fellowship*
Hath put awey, as thilke same,   *excluded*
Which lustles ferr from alle game
In chambre doth fulofte wo
Abedde, whanne it falleth so
That love sholde ben awaited.

But Slowthe, which is evele affaited,   misshapen
With Slep hath mad his retenue,   (1201)
That what thing is to Love due,
Of all his dette he payeth non:
He wot noght how the niht is gon
Ne hou the day is come aboute,
Bot only forto slepe and route   snore
Til hih midday, that he arise.
Bot Cephalus dede otherwise,
As thou, my sone, hast herd above.

A: My fader, who that hath his love   (1210)
Abedde naked be his side,
And wolde thanne hise yhen hide
With slep, I not what man is he:
Bot certes as touchende of me,
That fell me nevere yit er this.
Bot otherwhile, whan so is
That I may cacche slep on honde
Liggende al one, thanne I fonde   endeavour
To dreme a merye swevene er day;
And if so falle that I may   (1220)
My thought with such a swevene plese,
Me thenkth I am somdiel in ese,
For I non other confort have.
So nedeth noght that I shal crave
The sonnes carte forto tarye,
Ne yit the mone, that she carye
Hire cours along upon the hevene,
For I am noght the more in evene
Towardes love in no degree:
Bot in my slep yit thanne I se   (1230)
Somwhat in swevene of that me liketh,
Which afterward myn herte entriketh,   misleads

110

Whan that I finde it otherwise.
So wot I noght of what servise
That Slep to mannes ese doth.

*   *   *

BOOK FIVE

Amans:
My fader, for that ye nou telle,
I have herd ofte time telle
Of Jelousye, bot what it is
Yit understod I nevere er this:
Wherfore I wolde you beseche,
That ye me wolde enforme and teche
What maner thing it mihte be.

Confessor:
My sone, that is hard to me:
Bot natheles, as I have herd,
Now herkne and thou shalt ben ansuerd.   (10)

    Among the men lacke of manhode
In mariage upon wifhode
Makth that a man himself deceiveth,
Wherof it is that he conceiveth
That ilke unsely maladye,   unhappy
The which is cleped Jelousye:
Of which if I the proprete
Shal telle after the nicete,
So as it worcheth on a man,
A fievere it is cotidian,   unceasing
Which every day wol come aboute,   (21)
Wher so a man be inne or oute.
At hom if that man wol wone,
This fievere is thanne of comun wone   custom
Most grevous in a mannes yhe:
For thanne he makth him tote and pryhe,   spy
Wher so as evere his love go;
She shal noght with hir litel too

Misteppe, bot he se it al.
His yhe is walkende overal;   (30)
Wher that she singe or that she dance,
He seth the leste contienance,   expression
If she loke on a man aside
Or with him roune at eny tide,   whisper
Or that she lawghe, or that she loure,   frowns
His yhe is ther at every houre.
And whanne it draweth to the niht,
If she thanne is withoute liht,
Anon is al the game shent;   ruined
For thanne he set his parlement   council
To speke it whan he comth to bedde,   (41)
And seith, 'If I were now to wedde,
I wolde neveremore have wif.'
And so he torneth into strif
The lust of loves duete,
And al upon diversete.   perversity
If she be freish and wel arayed,
He seith hir baner is displayed
To clepe in gestes fro the weye: call
And if she be noght wel beseye,   dressed
And that hir list noght to be gladd,   (51)
He berth an hond that she is madd
And loveth noght hire housebonde;
He seith he may wel understonde,
That if she wolde his compaignye,
She sholde thanne afore his ye
Shewe al the plesir that she mihte.
So that be daye ne be nihte
She not what thing is for the beste,
Bot liveth out of alle reste;   (60)
For what as evere him liste sein,
She dar noght speke a word ayein,

Bot wepth and holt hire lippes clos.
She may wel write, 'Sanz repos,'   without rest
The wif which is to such on maried.
    Of alle wommen be he waried,   cursed
For with this fievere of jalousye
His echedayes fantasye
Of sorghe is evere aliche grene,   similarly
So that ther is no love sene,   (70)
Whil that him list at hom abide.
And whan so is he wol out ride,
Thanne hath he redy his aspye
Abidinge in hir compaignye,
A janglere, an evel mouthed oon,
That she ne may nowhider gon,
Ne speke a word, ne ones loke,
That he ne wol it wende and croke   turn; distort
And torne after his oghne entente,
Thogh she nothing bot honour mente.   (80)
Whan that the lord comth hom ayein,
The janglere moste somwhat sein;
So what withoute and what withinne,
This fievere is evere to beginne,
For where he comth he can noght ende,
Til death of him have mad an ende.
For thogh so be that he ne hiere
Ne se ne wite in no manere   find out
Bot al honour and wommanhiede,
Therof the jelous takth non hiede,   (90)
Bot as a man to love unkinde,
He cast his staf, as doth the blinde,
And fint defaulte where is non;
As who so dremeth on a ston
Hou he is leid, and groneth ofte,
Whan he lith on his pilwes softe.

114

So is ther noght bot strif and cheste;
Whan love sholde make his feste,
It is gret thing if he hir kisse:
Thus hath she lost the nihtes blisse, (100)
For at such time he gruccheth evere complains
And berth on hond there is a levere, asserts; dearer one
And that she wolde an other were
In stede of him abedde there;
And with tho wordes and with mo
Of jelousye he torneth fro
And lith upon his other side,
And she with that drawth hire aside,
And ther she wepeth al the niht.
Ha, to what peine she is diht, destined
That in hire youthe hath so beset (111)
The bond which may noght ben unknet!
I wot the time is ofte cursed,
That evere was the gold unpursed,
The which was leid upon the bok,
Whan that alle othre she forsok
For love of him; bot al to late
She pleigneth, for as thanne algate in any case
She mot forbere and to him bowe,
Thogh he ne wole it noght allowe. (120)
For man is lord of thilke feire, far one
So may the womman bot empeire,
If she speke oght ayein his wille;
And thus she berth hir peine stille.

    Bot if this fievere a womman take,
She shal be wel mor harde shake;
For thogh she bothe se and hiere,
And finde that ther is matiere,
She dar bot to hirselve pleine,
And thus she suffreth double peine. (130)

Lo thus, my sone, as I have write,
Thou miht of Jelousye wite   know
His fievere and his condicion,
Which is full of suspecion.
Bot wherof that this fievere groweth,
Who so these olde bokes troweth,
Ther may he finden hou it is:
For they ous teche and telle this,
Hou that this fievere of jelousye
Somdel it groweth of sotye   folly
Of love, and somdiel of untrust.   (141)
For as a sek man lest his lust,
And whan he may no savour gete,
He hateth thanne his oughne mete,
Riht so this fieverous maladye,
Which caused is of fantasye,
Makth the jelous in fieble plit
To lese of love his appetit
Thurgh feigned enformacion
Of his imaginacion.   (150)

   Bot finaly to taken hiede,
Men may wel make a liklihiede   comparison
Betwen him which is averous
Of gold and him that is jelous
Of love, for in on degre
They stonde bothe, as semeth me.
That oon wolde have his bagges stille,   one
And noght departen with his wille,   pleasure
And dar noght for the thieves slepe,
So fain he wolde his tresor kepe;   (160)
That other may noght wel be glad,
For he is evere more adrad
Of these lovers that gon aboute,
In aunter if they putte him oute.   in case that

So have they bothe litel joye
As wel of love as of monoye.
    Now hast thou, sone, at my techinge
Of Jelousye a knowlechinge,
That thou miht understonde this,
Fro whenne he comth and what he is,   (170)
And ek to whom that he is lik.
Be war forthy thou be noght sik
Of thilke fievere as I have spoke,
For it wol in himself be wroke.
For Love hateth nothing more,
As men may finde be the lore
Of hem that whilom were wise,
Hou that they spieke in many wise.

A: My fader, soth is that ye sein.
Bot forto loke therayein,
Befor this time hou it is falle,   (180)
Wherof ther mihte ensample falle
To suche men as be jelous
In what manere it is grevous,
Riht fain I wolde ensample hiere.

C: My goode sone, at thy preyere
Of suche ensamples as I finde,
So as they comen nou to minde
Upon this point, of time gon
I thenke forto tellen on.   (190)

    Ovide wrot of many thinges,
Among the whiche in his writinges
He tolde a tale in poesye,
Which toucheth unto Jelousye,
Upon a certein cas of love.

Among the goddes alle above
It fell at thilke time thus:
The god of Fir, which Vulcanus   Fire
Is hote, and hath a craft forthwith   called
Assigned, forto be the smith   (200)
Of Jupiter, and his figure
Bothe of visage and of stature
Is lothly and malgracious,
Bot yit he hath withinne his hous
As for the likinge of his lif
The faire Venus to his wif.
Bot Mars, which of batailles is
The god, an yhe hadde unto this:
As he which was chivalerous,
It fell him to ben amerous,   (210)
And thoghte it was a gret pite
To se so lusty on as she
Be coupled with so lourde a wiht: dull
So that his peine day and niht
He ded, if he hire winne mihte;
And she, which hadde a good insihte
Toward so noble a knihtly lord,
In love fell of his acord.
Ther lacketh noght bot time and place,
That he nis siker of hire grace: certain
Bot whan tuo hertes falle in on,   (221)
So wis await was nevere non,
That at som time they ne mete;
And thus this faire lusty swete
With Mars hath ofte compaignye.
Bot thilke unkinde Jelousye,
Which everemor the herte opposeth,
Makth Vulcanus that he supposeth
That it is noght wel overal,

And to himself he seide, he shal (230)
Aspye betre, if that he may;
And so it fell upon a day,
That he this thing so slyhly ledde,
He fonde hem bothe tuo abedde
Al warm, echon with other naked.
And he with craft al redy maked
Of stronge chenes hath hem bounde,
As he togedre hem hadde founde,
And lefte hem bothe ligge so,
And gan to clepe and crye tho (240)
Unto the goddes al aboute;
And they assembled in a route
Come alle at ones forto se.
Bot none amendes hadde he,
Bot was rebuked hiere and there
Of hem that Loves frendes were;
And seiden that he was to blame,
For if ther fell him eny shame,
It was thurgh his misgovernance:
And thus he lost contienance, (250)
This god, and let his cause falle;
And they to skorne him lowhen alle,   laughed
And losen Mars out of hise bondes.
Wherof these erthly housebondes
For evere mihte ensample take,
If such a chaunce hem overtake:
For Vulcanus his wif bewreide,   exposed
The blame upon himself he leide,
Wherof his shame was the more;
Which oghte forto ben a lore (260)
For every man that liveth hiere,
To reulen him in this matiere.
Thogh such an happ of love asterte,

119

Yit sholde he noght apointe his herte
With jelousye of that is wroght,
Bot feigne, as thogh he wiste it noght:
For if he lete it overpasse,
The slaundre shal be wel the lasse,
And he the more in ese stonde.
For this thou miht wel understonde,   (270)
That where a man shal nedes lese,
The leste harme is forto chese.
Bot Jelousye of his untrist
Makth that full many an harm arist,
Which elles sholde noght arise;
And if a man him wolde avise
Of that befell to Vulcanus,
Him oghte of reson thenke thus,
That sithe a god therof was shamed,
Wel sholde an erthly man be blamed   (280)
To take upon him such a vice.
　　Forthy, my sone, in thin office
Be war that thou be noght jelous,
Which ofte time hath shent the house.   ruined

*　　　*　　　*

　　In the lignage of Avarice,
My sone, yit ther is a vice,
His righte name it is Ravine,   Rapine
Which hath a route of his covine.   troop; confederates
Ravine among the maistres duelleth,
And with his servantz, as men telleth,   (290)
Extorcion is nou withholde: in service
Ravine of othre mennes folde   flock
Makth his larder and payeth noght;

For wher as evere it may be soght,
In his hous ther shal nothing lacke,
And that fulofte abith the packe   pays for
Of povere men that duelle aboute.
Thus stant the comun poeple in doute,
Which can do non amendement;
For whanne him faileth payement,   (300)
Ravine makth non other skile,
Bot takth be strengthe what he wile.
    So ben ther in the same wise
Lovers, as I thee shal devise,
That whan noght elles may availe,
Anon with strengthe they assaile
And gete of love the sesine,   possession
Whan they se time, be ravine.
    Forthy, my sone, shrif thee hier,
If thou hast ben a raviner   (310)
Of love.

A: Certes, fader, no:
For I my lady love so,
That thogh I were as was Pompeye,
That al the world me wolde obeye,
Or elles such as Alisandre,
I wolde noght do such a sklaundre;
It is no good man, which so doth.

C: In good feith, sone, thou seist soth:
For he that wole of pourveance   foresight
Be such a weye his luste avance,   (321)
He shal it after sore abye,
Bot if these olde ensamples lie.

121

A: Nou, goode fader, tell me on,
So as ye cunne manyon,   know
Touchende of love in this matiere.

C: Nou liste, my sone, and thou shalt hiere,
So as it hath befalle er this,
In loves cause hou that it is
A man to take be ravine   (330)
The preye which is femeline.   female

   Ther was a real noble king,   royal
And riche of alle worldes thing,
Which of his propre enheritance
Athenes hadde in governance,
And who so thenke therupon,
His name was king Pandion.
Tuo douhtres hadde he be his wif,
The whiche he lovede as his lif;
The ferste douhter Progne hihte,   (340)
And the secounde, as she wel mihte,
Was cleped faire Philomene,
To whom fell after mochel tene.   trouble
The fader of his pourveance
His doughter Progne wolde avance,
And yaf hire unto mariage
A worthy king of hih lignage,
A noble kniht eke of his hond,
So was he kid in every lond,   known
Of Trace he hihte Tereus;   (350)
The clerk Ovide telleth thus.
This Tereus his wif hom ladde,
A lusty lif with hire he hadde;
Til it befell upon a tide,
This Progne, as she lay him beside,

Bethoughte hir hou it mihte be
That she hir soster mihte se,
And to hir lord hir will she seide,
With goodly wordes and him preide
That she to hire mihte go: (360)
And if it liked him noght so,
That thanne he wolde himselve wende,
Of elles be som other sende,
Which mihte hire diere soster griete,
And shape hou that they mihten miete.
Hir lord anon to that he herde
Yaf his acord, and thus ansuerde:
'I wole,' he seide, 'for thy sake
The weye after thy soster take
Myself, and bringe hire, if I may.'   (370)
And she with that, there as he lay,
Began him in hire armes clippe,
And kist him with hir softe lippe,
And seide, 'Sire, grant mercy.'
And he sone after was redy,
And tok his leve forto go;
In sory time dede he so.
    This Tercus goth forth to shipe
With him and with his felashipe;
Be see the rihte cours he nam,   (380)
Into the contre til he cam,
Wher Philomene was duellinge,
And of hir soster the tidinge
He tolde, and tho they weren glade,
And mochel joye of him they made.
The fader and the moder bothe
To leve here douhter weren lothe,
Bot if they weren in presence;
And natheles at reverence

Of him, that wolde himself travaile,   (390)
They wolden noght he sholde faile
Of that he preide, and yive hire leve:
And she, that wolde noght beleve,   linger
In alle haste made hire yare   ready
Toward hir soster forto fare,
With Tereus and forth she wente.
And he with al his hole entente,
Whan she was fro hir frendes go,
Assoteth of hire love so,   was besotted
His yhe mihte he noght withholde,   (400)
That he ne moste on hir beholde;
And with the sihte he gan desire,
And sette his oghne herte on fire;
And fir, whan it to tow aprocheth,   hemp
To him anon the strengthe acrocheth,   gathers
Til with his hete it be devoured,
The tow ne may noght be socoured.
And so that tyrant raviner,
Whan that she was in his pouer,
And he therto sawh time and place,   (410)
As he that lost hath alle grace,
Foryat he was a wedded man,
And in a rage on hire he ran,
Riht as a wolf which takth his preye.
And she began to crye and preye,
'O fader, o my moder diere,
Nou helpe!' Bot they ne mihte it hiere,
And she was of to litel miht
Defense ayein so ruide a kniht
To make, whanne he was so wod,   mad
That he no reson understod,   (421)
Bot hield hire under in such wise,
That she ne mihte noght arise,

Bot lay oppressed and desesed,   suffering
As if a goshauk hadde sesed
A brid, which dorste noght for fere
Remue: and thus this tyrant there   move
Beraft hire such thing as men sein
May neveremor be yolde ayein,   restored
And that was the virginite: (430)
Of such ravine it was pite.
    Bot whan she to hirselven com,
And of hir meschief hiede nom,
And knew hou that she was no maide,
With wofull herte thus she saide:
'O thou of alle men the worste,
Wher was ther evere man that dorste
Do such a dede as thou hast do?
That day shal falle, I hope so,
That I shal telle out al my fille,   (440)
And with my speche I shal fulfille
The wide world in brede and lengthe.
That thou hast do to me be strengthe,
If I among the poeple duelle,
Unto the poeple I shal it telle;
And if I be withinne wall
Of stones closed, thanne I shal
Unto the stones clepe and crye,   call
And tellen hem thy felonye;
And if to the wodes wende,   (450)
Ther shal I tellen tale and ende,   the whole story
And crye it to the briddes oute,
That they shul hiere it al aboute.
For I so loude it shal reherce,
That my vois shal the hevene perce,
That it shal soune in Goddes ere.
Ha, false man, where is thy fere?

125

O mor cruel than eny beste,
Hou hast thou holden thy beheste
Which thou unto my soster madest?   (460)
O thou, which alle love ungladest,   distresses
And art ensample of alle untrewe,
Nou wolde God my soster knewe,
Of thin untrouthe, hou that it stod!'
And he than as a lyon wod
With hise unhappy handes stronge   ill-fortuned
Hire cauhte be the tresses longe,
With whiche he bond ther bothe hire armes,
That was a fieble ded of armes,
And to the grounde anon hire caste,   (470)
And out he clippeth also faste
Hire tunge with a peire sheres.
So what with blod and what with teres
Out of hire yhe and of hir mouth,
He made hire faire face uncouth: inrecognizable
She lay swounende unto the deth,
Ther was unethes eny breth;   scarcely
Bot yit whan he hire tunge refte,
A litel part therof belefte,
Bot she with al no word may soune,   (480)
Bot chitre and as a brid jargoune.   chatter
And natheles that wode hound
Hir body hent up fro the ground,   seized
And sente hir there as be his wille
She sholde abide in prison stille
For everemo: bot nou tak hiede
What after fell of this misdede.
    Whanne al this meschief was befalle,
This Tereus, that foule him falle,   may evil befall
Unto his contre hom he tih;   went
And whan he com his paleis nih,   (491)

126

His wif al redy there him kepte.
Whan he hir sih, anon he wepte,
And that he dede for deceite,
For she began to axe him streite,
'Wher is my soster?' And he seide
That she was ded; and Progne abreide,　　　　　　　started up
As she that was a wofull wif,
And stod betuen hire deth and lif,
Of that she herde such tidinge:　　　　　　　　　　(500)
Bot for she sih hire lord wepinge,
She wende noght bot alle trouthe,
And hadde wel the more routhe.　　　　　　　　　sorrow
The perles weren tho forsake
To hire, and blake clothes take;
As she that was gentil and kinde,
In worshipe of hir sostres minde
She made a riche enterement,
For she fond non amendement
To sighen or to sobbe more:　　　　　　　　　　(510)
So was ther guile under the gore.　　　　　　deceit; cloak
　　Nou leve we this king and queene,
And torne ayein to Philomene,
As I began to tellen erst,　　　　　　　　　　at first
Whan she cam into prison ferst,
It thoghte a kinges douhter strange
To maken so soudein a change
Fro welthe unto so grete a wo;
And she began to thenke tho,
Thogh she be mouthe nothing preide,　　　　　　(520)
Withinne hir herte thus she seide:
'O thou, almihty Jupiter,
That hihe sist and lokest fer,　　　　　　　　sits
Thou soffrest many a wrong doinge,
And yit it is noght thy willinge.

127

To thee ther may nothing ben hid,
Thou wost hou it is me betid:
I wolde I hadde noght be bore,   born
For thanne I hadde noght forlore   lost
My speche and my virginite.   (530)
Bot, goode lord, al is in thee,
Whan thou therof wolt do vengance
And shape my deliverance.'
And evere among this lady wepte,
And thoghte that she nevere kepte   cared
To ben a worldes womman more,
And that she wisheth everemore.
Bot ofte unto hir soster diere
Hire herte spekth in this manere,
And seide, 'Ha, soster, if ye knewe   (540)
Of myn astat, ye wolde rewe,
I trowe, and my deliverance
Ye wolde shape, and do vengance
On him that is so fals a man:
And natheles, so as I can,
I wol you sende som tokninge,
Wherof ye shul have knowlechinge
Of thing I wot, that shal you lothe,
The which you toucheth and me bothe.'
And tho withinne a whyle als tit   at once
She waf a cloth of selk al whit   (551)
With letres and imagerye,
In which was al the felonye
Which Tereus to hire hath do;
And lappede it togedre tho   folded
And sette hir signet therupon
And sende it unto Progne anon.
The messager which forth it bar,
What it amonteth is noght war;

And natheles to Progne he goth   (560)
And prively takth hire the cloth,
And wente ayein riht as he cam,
The court of him non hiede nam.
 Whan Progne of Philomene herde,
She wolde knowe hou that it ferde,
And opneth that the man hath broght,
And wot therby what hath be wroght
And what meschief ther is befalle.
In swoune tho she gan doun falle,
And efte aros and gan to stonde,   then
And eft she takth the cloth on honde,   (571)
Behield the lettres and thimages;
Bot ate laste, 'Of suche oultrages,'
She seith, 'wepinge is noght the bote:'   remedy
And swerth, if that she live mote,
It shal be venged otherwise.
And with that she gan hire avise
Hou ferst she mihte unto hire winne
Hir soster, that noman withinne,
Bot only they that were suore,   (580)
It sholde knowe, and shop therfore
That Tereus nothing it wiste;
And yit riht as hirselven liste,   desired
Hir soster was delivered sone   at once
Out of prison, and be the mone
To Progne she was broght be nihte.
 Whan ech of other hadde a sihte,
In chambre, ther they were al one,
They maden many a pitous mone;
Bot Progne most of sorwe made,   (590)
Which sihe hir soster pale and fade
And specheles and deshonoured,
Of that she hadde be defloured;

129

And ek upon hir lord she thoghte,
Of that he so untreuly wroghte
And hadde his espousaile broke.
She makth a vou it shal be wroke,   avenged
And with that word she kneleth doun
Wepinge in gret devocioun:
Unto Cupide and to Venus   (600)
She preide, and seide thanne thus:
'O ye, to whom nothing asterte   escape
Of love may, for every herte
Ye knowe, as ye that ben above
The god and the goddesse of Love;
Ye witen wel that evere yit   know
With al my will and al my wit,
Sith ferst ye shopen me to wedde,
That I lay with my lord abedde,
I have be trewe in my degre,   (610)
And evere thoghte forto be,
And nevere love in other place,
Bot al only the king of Trace,
Which is my lord and I his wif.
Bot nou allas this wofull strif!
That I him thus ayeinward finde   in return
The most untrewe and most unkinde
That evere in lady armes lay.
And wel I wot that he ne may
Amende his wrong, it is so gret;   (620)
For he to litel of me let,   regarded
Whan he myn oughne soster tok,
And me that am his wif forsok.'
    Lo, thus to Venus and Cupide
She preide, and furthermor she cride
Unto Appollo the hiheste,
And seide, 'O mighty god of Reste,

Thou do vengance of this debat.   dispute
My soster and al hire astat
Thou wost, and hou she hath forlore   (630)
Hir maidenhod, and I therfore
In al the world shal bere a blame
Of that my soster hath a shame,
That Tereus to hire I sente:
And wel thou wost that myn entente
Was al for worshipe and for goode.
O lord, that yifst the lives fode
To every wiht, I prey thee hiere
Thes wofull sostres that ben hiere,
And let ous noght to the ben lothe;   (640)
We ben thin oghne wommen bothe.'

    Thus pleigneth Progne and axeth wreche,   vengeance
And thogh hire soster lacke speche,
To him that alle thinges wot
Hire sorwe is noght the lasse hot:
Bot he that thanne had herd hem tuo,
Him oughte have sorwed everemo
For sorwe which was hem betuene.
With signes pleigneth Philomene,   (649)
And Progne seith, 'It shal be wreke,   avenged
That al the world therof shal speke.'
And Progne tho seknesse feigneth,
Wherof unto hir lord she pleigneth,
And preith she moste hire chambres kepe,
And as hir liketh wake and slepe.
And he hire granteth to be so;
And thus togedre ben they tuo,
That wolde him bot a litel good.
Nou herk hierafter hou it stod   (659)
Of wofull auntres that befelle: events
Thes sostres, that ben bothe felle,—   wrathful

And that was noght on hem along.   not their fault
Bot onliche on the grete wrong
Which Tereus hem hadde do,—
They shopen forto venge hem tho.
    This Tereus be Progne his wif
A sone hath, which as his lif
He loveth, and Ithis he hihte:
His moder wiste wel she mihte
Do Tereus no more grief   (670)
Than sle this child, which was so lief.
Thus she, that was, as who seith, mad
Of wo, which hath hir overlad,
Withoute insihte of moderhede
Foryat pite and loste drede,
And in hir chambre prively
This child withouten noise or cry
She slou, and hieu him al to pieces:
And after with diverse spieces
The fleish, whan it was so toheewe,   (680)
She takth, and makth therof a sewe,   stew
With which the fader at his mete
Was served, til he hadde him ete;
That he ne wiste hou that it stod,
Bot thus his oughne fleish and blod
Himself devoureth ayein kinde,
As he that was tofore unkinde.
And thanne, er that he were arise,
For that he sholde ben agrise,   horrified
To shewen him the child was ded,   (690)
This Philomene tok the hed
Betwen tuo dishes, and al wrothe
Tho comen forth the sostres bothe,
And setten it upon the bord.
And Progne tho began the word,

132

And seide, 'O werste of alle wicke,
Of conscience whom no pricke
May stere, lo, what thou hast do!
Lo, hier ben nou we sostres tuo;
O raviner, lo hier thy preye,   (700)
With whom so falsliche on the weye
Thou hast thy tirannye wroght.
Lo, nou it is somdel aboght,   paid for
And bet it shal, for of thy dede
The world shal evere singe and rede
In remembrance of thy defame:
For thou to love hast do such shame,
That it shal nevere be foryete.'
With that he sterte up fro the mete,   food
And shof the bord unto the flor,   (710)
And cauhte a swerd anon and suor
That they sholde of his handes die.
And they unto the goddes crye
Begunne with so loude a stevene,   voice
That they were herd unto the hevene;
And in a twinclinge of an yhe
The goddes, that the meschief sihe,
Here formes changen alle thre.
Echon of hem in his degre
Was torned into briddes kinde;   (720)
Diverseliche, as men may finde,
After thastat that they were inne,
Here formes were set atwinne.   apart
And as it telleth in the tale,
The ferst into a nihtingale
Was shape, and that was Philomene,
Which in the winter is noght sene,
For thanne ben the leves falle
And naked ben the buishes alle.

For after that she was a brid, (730)
Hir will was evere to ben hid,
And forto duelle in prive place,
That noman sholde sen hir face
For shame, which may noght be lassed, made less
Of thing that was tofore passed,
Whan that she loste hir maidenhiede:
For evere upon hir wommanhiede,
Thogh that the goddes wolde hire change,
She thenkth, and is the more strange,
And halt hir clos the wintres day. (740)
Bot whan the winter goth away,
And that Nature the goddesse
Wole of hir oughne fre largesse
With herbes and with floures bothe
The feldes and the medwes clothe,
And ek the wodes and the greves groves
Ben heled al with grene leves, covered
So that a brid hire hide may,
Betwen Averil and March and May,
She that the winter hield hir clos, (750)
For pure shame and noght aros,
Whan that she seth the bowes thikke,
And that ther is no bare sticke,
Bot al is hid with leves grene,
To wode comth this Philomene
And makth hir ferste yeres fliht;
Wher as she singeth day and niht,
And in hir song al openly
She makth hir pleignte and seith, 'O why,
O why ne were I yit a maide?' (760)
For so these olde wise saide,
Which understoden what she mente,
Hire notes ben of such entente.

And ek they seide hou in hir song
She makth gret joye and merthe among,
And seith, 'Ha, nou I am a brid,
Ha, nou my face may ben hid:
Thogh I have lost my maidenhede,
Shal noman se my chekes rede.'
Thus medleth she with joye wo   (770)
And with hir sorwe merthe also,
So that of loves maladye
She makth diverse melodye,
And seith love is a wofull blisse,
A wisdom which can noman wisse,   understand
A lusty fievere, a wounde softe:
This note she reherceth ofte
To hem whiche understonde hir tale.
Nou have I of this nihtingale,
Which erst was cleped Philomene,   (780)
Told al that evere I wolde mene,
Bothe of hir forme and of hir note,
Wherof men may the storye note.

    And of hir soster Progne I finde,
Hou she was torned out of kinde
Into a swalwe swift of winge,
Which ek in winter lith swouninge,
Ther as she may nothing be sene:
Bot whan the world is woxe grene
And comen is the somertide,   (790)
Than fleth she forth and ginth to chide,
And chitreth out in hir langage
What falshod is in mariage,
And telleth in a maner speche
Of Tereus the spousebreche.   adultery
She wol noght in the wodes duelle,
For she wolde openliche telle;

And ek for that she was a spouse,
Among the folk she comth to house,
To do thes wives understonde (800)
The falshod of hire housebonde,
That they of hem be war also,
For ther ben manye untrewe of tho.
Thus ben the sostres briddes bothe,
And ben toward the men so lothe,
That they ne wole of pure shame
Unto no mannes hand be tame;
For evere it duelleth in here minde
Of that they founde a man unkinde,
And that was false Tereus. (810)
If such on be amonges ous
I not, bot his condicion
Men sein in every region
Withinne toune and ek withoute
Nou regneth comunliche aboute.
And natheles in remembrance
I wol declare what vengance
The goddes hadden him ordeined,
Of that the sostres hadden pleigned:
For anon after he was changed (820)
And from his oghne kinde stranged,
A lappewincke mad he was,
And thus he hoppeth on the gras,
And on his hed ther stant upriht
A creste in tokne he was a kniht;
And yit unto this day men seith,
A lappewincke hath lore his feith   lost
And is the brid falseste of alle.
    Bewar, my sone, er thee so falle;
For if thou be of such covine,   conspiracy
To gete of love be ravine (831)

Thy lust, it may thee falle thus,
As it befell of Tereus.

A: My fader, goddes forebode!
Me were lever be fortrode   trampled
With wilde hors and be todrawe,
Er I ayein Love and his lawe
Dede eny thing or loude or stille,
Which were noght my lady wille.
Men sein that every love hath drede;   (840)
So folweth it that I hire drede,
For I hire love, and who so dredeth,
To plese his love and serve him nedeth.
Thus may ye knowen be this skile   reason
That no ravine don I wile
Ayein hir will be such a weye;
Bot while I live, I wol obeye
Abidinge on hire courtesye
If eny mercy wolde hir plye.   bend
Forthy, my fader, as of this   (850)
I wot noght I have don amis:
Bot furthermore I you beseche,
Som other point that ye me teche,
And axeth forth, if ther be auht,
That I may be the betre tauht.

*   *   *

BOOK SIX

Confessor:
Who dar do thing which Love ne dar?
To Love is every lawe unwar,   unknown
Bot to the lawes of his heste   command
The fish, the foul, the man, the beste
Of al the worldes kinde louteth.   bows
For Love is he which nothing douteth;
In mannes herte where he sit,
He compteth noght toward his wit
The wo nomore than the wele,
No mor the hete than the chele,   (10)
No mor the wete than the dreye,
No mor to live than to deie,
So that tofore ne behinde
He seth nothing, bot as the blinde
Withoute insihte of his corage
He doth merveilles in his rage.
To what thing that he wole him drawe,
Ther is no god, ther is no lawe,
Of whom that he takth eny hiede;
Bot as Bayard the blinde stede,   horse
Til he falle in the dich amidde,   (21)
He goth ther noman wole him bidde;
He stant so ferforth out of reule,
Ther is no Wit that may him reule.
And thus to telle of him in soth,
Ful many a wonder thing he doth,
That were betre to be laft,
Among the whiche is wichecraft,
That som men clepen Sorcerye,
Which forto winne his druerye   beloved
With many a circumstance he useth, (31)

Ther is no point which he refuseth.

*   *   *

   Among hem whiche at Troye were,
Uluxes ate siege there
Was on be name in special;
Of whom yit the memorial
Abit, for whil ther is a mouth,
For evere his name shal be couth.   known
He was a worthy kniht and king
And clerk knowende of every thing;   (40)
He was a gret rethorien,
He was a gret magicien;
Of Tullius the rethorique,
Of king Zorastes the magique,
Of Tholome thastronomye,
Of Plato the philosophye,
Of Daniel the slepy dremes,
Of Neptune ek the water stremes,
Of Salomon and the proverbes,
Of Macer al the strengthe of herbes,   (50)
And the phisique of Ypocras,   Hippocrates
And lich unto Pictagoras
Of surgerye he knew the cures.
Bot somwhat of his aventures,
Which shal to my matiere acorde,
To thee, my sone, I wol recorde.
   This king, of which thou hast herd sein,
Fro Troye as he goth hom ayein
Be shipe, he fond the see divers,
With many a windy storm revers.   (60)
Bot he thurgh wisdom that he shapeth

Ful many a gret peril ascapeth,
Of whiche I thenke tellen on,
Hou that malgre the nedle and ston   despite
Winddrive he was al soudeinly
Upon the strondes of Cilly,   Sicily
Wher that he moste abide a while.
Tuo queenes weren in that ile
Calipsa named and Circes;
And whan they herde hou Uluxes   (70)
Is londed ther upon the rive,   shore
For him they senden als so blive.   quickly
With him suche as he wolde he nam
And to the court to hem he cam.
Thes queenes were as tuo goddesses
Of art magique sorceresses,
That what lord comth to that rivage,   coast
They make him love in such a rage
And upon hem assote so,   dote
That they wol have, er that he go,   (80)
Al that he hath of worldes good.
Uluxes wel this understod,
They couthe moche, he couthe more;
They shape and caste ayein him sore
And wroghte many a soutil wile,
Bot yit they mihte him noght beguile.
Bot of the men of his navye
They tuo forshope a gret partye,
May non of hem withstonde here hestes;
Som part they shopen into bestes,   (90)
Som part they shopen into foules;   birds
To beres, tigres, apes, oules,
Or elles, be som other weye;
Ther mihte hem nothing desobeye,
Such craft they hadde above kinde.

Bot that art couthe they noght finde,
Of which Uluxes was deceived,
That he ne hath hem alle weived,   put aside
And broght hem into such a rote,   state
That upon him they bothe assote;   (100)
And thurgh the science of his art
He tok of hem so wel his part,
That he begat Circes with childe.
He kepte him sobre and made hem wilde,
He sette himselve so above,
That with here good and with here love,
Who that therof be lief or loth,
Al quit into his ship he goth.
Circes toswolle bothe sides
He lefte, and waiteth on the tides,   (110)
And straght thurghout the salte fom
He takth his cours and comth him hom,
Where as he fond Penolope;
A betre wif ther may non be,
And yit ther ben inowhe of goode.
Bot who hir goodshipe understode
Fro ferst that she wifhode tok,
Hou many loves she forsok
And hou she bar hire al aboute,
Ther whiles that hire lord was oute,   (120)
He mihte make a gret avant   boast
Amonges al the remenant
That she was on of al the beste.
Wel mihte he sette his herte in reste,
This king, whan he hir fond in hele;
For as he couthe in wisdom dele,
So couthe she in wommanhiede:
And whan she sih withoute drede
Hire lord upon his oghne ground,

141

That he was come sauf and sound,   (130)
In al this world ne mihte be
A gladdere womman than was she.
  The fame, which may noght ben hidd,
Thurghout the lond is sone kidd,   proclaimed
Here king is come hom ayein:
Ther may noman the fulle sein,
Hou that they weren alle glade,
So mochel joye of him they made.
The presens every day be newed,
He was with yiftes al besnewed;   (140)
The poeple was of him so glad,
That thogh non other man hem bad,
Taillage upon hemself they sette,   taxation
And as it were of pure dette
They yeve here goodes to the king:
This was a glad hom welcoming.
Thus hath Uluxes what he wolde,
His wif was such as she be sholde,
His poeple was to him sougit,   subject
Him lacketh nothing of delit.   (150)
  Bot Fortune is of such a sleihte,   skill
That whan a man is most on heihte,
She makth him rathest forto falle: quickest
Ther wot noman what shal befalle,
The happes over mannes hed
Ben honged with a tendre thred.
That proved was on Uluxes;
For whan he was most in his pes,
Fortune gan to make him werre
And sette his welthe al out of herre.   order
Upon a day as he was merye,   (161)
As thogh ther mihte him nothing derye,   harm
Whan niht was come, he goth to bedde,

With slep and bothe his yhen fedde.
And while he slepte, he mette a swevene:
Him thoghte he sih a stature evene,
Which brihtere than the sonne shon;
A man it semeth was it non,
Bot yit it was as in figure
Most lich to mannish creature,   (170)
Bot as of beaute hevenlich
It was most to an angel lich:
And thus betwen angel and man
Beholden it this king began,
And such a lust tok of the sihte,
That fain he wolde, if that he mihte,
The forme of that figure embrace;
And goth him forth toward the place,
Wher he sih that image tho,
And takth it in his armes tuo,   (180)
And it embraceth him ayein
And to the king thus gan it sein:
'Uluxes, understond wel this,
The tokne of oure aqueintance is
Hierafterward to mochel tene: sorrow
The love that is ous betuene,
Of that we nou such joye make,
That on of ous the deth shal take,
Whan time comth of destine;
It may non otherwise be.'   (190)
Uluxes tho began to preye
That this figure wolde him seye
What wiht he is that seith him so.
This wiht upon a spere tho
A pensel which was wel begon,   banner
Embrouded, sheweth him anon:
Thre fishes alle of o colour

143

In manere as it were a tour   *tower*
Upon the pensel were wroght.
Uluxes kneu this tokne noght,   (200)
And preith to wite in som partye   *know*
What thing it mihte signefye.
'A signe it is,' the wiht ansuerde,
'Of an empire:' and forth he ferde   *went*
Al sodeinly, whan he that seide.
    Uluxes out of slep abreide,
And that was riht ayein the day,   *towards*
That lengere slepen he ne may.
Men sein, a man hath knowleching
Save of himself of alle thing;   (210)
His oghne chance noman knoweth,
Bot as fortune it on him throweth:
Was nevere yit so wis a clerk,
Which mihte knowe al Goddes werk,
Ne the secret which God hath set
Ayein a man may noght be let.
Uluxes, thogh that he be wis,
With al his wit in his avis,
The mor that he his swevene acompteth,
The lasse he wot what it amonteth: (220)
For al his calculacion,
He seth no demonstracion
Al pleinly forto knowe an ende;
Bot natheles hou so it wende,
He dradde him of his oghne sone.
That makth him wel the more astone,   *upset*
And shop therfore anon withal,
So that withinne castel wall
Thelamachum his sone he shette,
And upon him strong warde he sette.   (230)
The sothe furthere he ne knew,

Til that Fortune him overthreu;
Bot natheles for sikernesse,
Wher that he mihte wite and gesse
A place strengest in his lond,
Ther let he make of lim and sond   lime
A strengthe where he wolde duelle;
Was nevere man yit herde telle
Of such an other as it was.
And forto strengthe him in that cas,   (240)
Of al his lond the sekereste
Of servantz and the worthieste,
To kepen him withinne warde,
He sette his body forto warde;
And made such an ordinance,
For love ne for aqueintance,
That were it erly, were it late,
They sholde lete in ate gate
No maner man, what so betidde,
Bot if so were himself it bidde.   (250)
    Bot al that mihte him noght availe,
For whom Fortune wole assaile,
Ther may be non such resistence,
Which mihte make a man defence;
Al that shal be mot falle algate.   anyway
This Circes, which I spak of late,
On whom Uluxes hath begete
A child, thogh he it have foryete,
Whan time com, as it was wone,   customary
She was delivered of a sone,   (260)
Which cleped is Thelogonus.
This child, whan he was bore thus,
Aboute his moder to ful age,
That he can reson and langage,
In good astat was drawe forth:

145

And whan he was so mochel worth
To stonden in a mannes stede,
Circes his moder hath him bede
That he shal to his fader go,
And tolde him al togedre tho   (270)
What man he was that him begat.
And whan Thelogonus of that
Was war and hath ful knowleching
Hou that his fader was a king,
He preith his moder faire this,
To go wher that his fader is;
And she him granteth that he shal,
And made him redy forth withal.
It was that time such usance,
That every man the conoiscance   cognizance
Of his contre bar in his hond,   (281)
Whan he wente into strange lond;
And thus was every man therfore
Wel knowe, wher that he was bore: born
For espiaile and mistrowinges   espionage; distrust
They dede thanne suche thinges,
That every man may other knowe.
So if befell that ilke throwe   time
Thelogonus as in this cas;
Of his contre the signe was   (290)
Thre fishes, whiche he sholde bere
Upon the penon of a spere: pennon
And whan that he was thus arrayed
And hath his harneis al assayed,
That he was redy everydel,
His moder bad him farewel,
And seide him that he sholde swithe   swiftly
His fader griete a thousand sithe.   times
        Thelogonus his moder kiste

146

And tok his leve, and wher he wiste   (300)
His fader was, the weye nam,
Til he unto Nachaie cam,
Which of that lond the chief cite
Was cleped, and ther axeth he
Wher was the king and hou he ferde.
And whan that he the sothe herde,
Wher that the king Uluxes was,
Al one upon his hors gret pas
He rod him forth, and in his hond
He bar the signal of his lond   (310)
With fishes thre, as I have told;
And thus he wente unto that hold,   stronghold
Wher that his oghne fader duelleth.
The cause why he comth he telleth
Unto the kepers of the gate,
And wolde have comen in therate,
Bot shortly they him seide nay:
And he als faire as evere he may
Besoghte and tolde hem ofte this,
Hou that the king his fader is;   (320)
Bot they with proude wordes grete
Begunne to manace and threte,
Bot he go fro the gate faste,
They wolde him take and sette faste.
Fro wordes unto strokes thus
They felle, and so Thelogonus
Was sore hurt and welnih ded;
Bot with his sharpe speres hed
He makth defence, hou so it falle,
And wan the gate upon hem alle,   (330)
And hath slain of the beste five;
And they ascriden als so blive   cried out
Thurghout the castell al aboute.

On every side men come oute,
Wherof the kinges herte afflihte,
And he with al the haste he mihte
A spere cauhte and out he goth,
As he that was nih wod for wroth.
He sih the gates ful of blod,
Thelogonus and wher he stod   (340)
He sih also, bot he ne knew
What man it was, and to him threw
His spere, and he sterte out aside.
Bot destine, which shal betide,
Befell that ilke time so,
Thelogonus knew nothing tho
What man it was that to him caste,
And while his oghne spere laste,
With al the signe therupon
He caste unto the king anon,   (350)
And smot him with a dedly wounde.
Uluxes fell anon to grounde;
Tho every man, 'The king! the king!'
Began to crye, and of this thing
Thelogonus, which sih the cas,
On knes he fell and seide, 'Helas!
I have min oghne fader slain:
Nou wolde I deie wonder fain,
Nou sle me who that evere wile,
For certes it is riht good skile.'   (360)
He crith, he wepth, he seith therfore,
'Helas, that evere was I bore,
That this unhappy destine
So wofully comth in be me!'
This king, which yit hath lif inouh,
His herte ayein to him he drouh,   drew
And to that vois an ere he leide

148

And understod al that he seide,
And gan to speke, and seide on hih,
'Bring me this man.' And whan he sih   (370)
Thelogonus, his thoght he sette
Upon the swevene which he mette,
And axeth that he mihte se
His spere, on which the fishes thre
He sih upon a pensel wroght.
Tho wiste he wel it faileth noght,
And badd him that he telle sholde
From whenne he cam and what he wolde.
    Thelogonus in sorghe and wo
So as he mihte tolde tho   (380)
Unto Uluxes al the cas,
Hou that Circes his moder was,
And so forth seide him everydel,
Hou that his moder gret him wel,
And in what wise she him sente.
Tho wiste Uluxes what it mente,
And tok him in hise armes softe,
And al bledende he kest him ofte,   kissed
And seide, 'sone, whil I love,
This infortune I thee foryive.'   (390)
After his other sone in haste
He sende, and he began him haste
And cam unto his fader tit.   quickly
Bot whan he sih him in such plit,
He wolde have ronne upon that other
Anon, and slain his oghne brother,
Ne hadde be that Uluxes
Betwen hem made acord and pes,
And to his heir Thelamachus
He bad that he Thelogonus   (400)
With al hi poure sholde kepe,

149

Til he were of his woundes depe
Al hol, and thanne he sholde him yive
Lond wher upon he mihte live.
Thelamachus, whan he this herde,
Unto his fader he ansuerde
And seide he wolde don his wille.
So duelle they togedre stille,
These brethren, and the fader sterveth.   dies
    Lo, wherof sorcerye serveth.   (410)
Thurgh sorcerye his lust he wan,
Thurgh sorcerye his wo began,
Thurgh sorcerye his love he ches,
Thurgh sorcerye his lif he les;
The child was gete in sorcerye,
The which dede al this felonye:
Thing which was ayein kinde wroght
Unkindeliche it was aboght;
The child his oghne fader slowh,
That was unkindeshipe inowh.   (420)
Forthy tak hiede hou that it is,
So forto winne love amis,
Which endeth al his joye in wo:

*   *   *

BOOK EIGHT

Confessor:
Lo thus, my sone, miht thou liere
What is to love in good manere,
And what to love in other wise:
The mede arist of the servise;
Fortune, thogh she be noght stable,
Yit at som time is favorable
To hem that ben of love trewe.
Bot certes it is forto rewe
To se love ayein kinde falle,   nature
For that makth sore a man to falle,   (10)
As thou miht of tofore rede.
Forthy, my sone, I wolde rede
To lete al other love aweye,
Bot if it be thurgh such a weye
As Love and Reson wolde acorde.
For elles, if that thou descorde,   differ
And take lust as doth a beste,
Thy love may noght ben honeste;
For be no skile that I finde
Such lust is noght of loves kinde.   (20)

Amans:
My fader, hou so that it stonde,
Youre tale is herd and understonde,
As thing which worthy is to hiere,
Of gret ensample and gret matiere,
Wherof, my fader, God you quite.   requite
Bot in this point myself aquite
I may riht wel, that nevere yit
I was assoted in my wit,   besotted
Bot only in that worthy place

Wher alle lust and alle grace (30)
Is set, if that Danger ne were.
Bot that is al my moste fere:
I not what ye fortune acompte, evaluate
Bot what thing Danger may amonte signify
I wot wel, for I have assayed;
For whan myn herte is best arrayed
And I have al my wit thurghsoght
Of love to beseche hire oght,
For al that evere I skile may,
I am concluded with a nay: (40)
That o sillable hath overthrowe
A thousend wordes on a rowe
Of suche as I best speke can;
Thus am I bot a lewed man. ignorant
Bot, fader, for ye ben a clerk
Of love, and this matiere is derk,
And I can evere leng the lasse,
Bot yit I may noght let it passe,
Youre hole conseil I beseche,
That ye me be som weye teche (50)
What is my beste, as for an ende.

C: My sone, unto the trouthe wende
Now wol I for the love of thee,
And lete alle othre truffles be. trifles

   The more that the nede is hih,
The more it nedeth to be slyh
To him which hath the nede on honde.
I have wel herd and understonde,
My sone, al that thou hast me seid,
And ek of that thou hast me preid, (60)
Nou at this time that I shal

As for conclusioun final
Conseile upon thy nede sette:
So thenke I finaly to knette
This cause, where it is tobroke,
And make an ende of that is spoke.
For I behihte thee that yifte   *promised*
Ferst whan thou come under my shrifte,
That thogh I toward Venus were,   *in attendance on*
Yit spak I suche wordes there,   *(70)*
That for the presthod which I have,
Myn ordre and myn astate to save,
I seide I wolde of myn office
To vertu more than to vice
Encline, and teche thee my lore.
Forthy to speken overmore
Of love, which thee may availe,
Tak love where it may noght faile:
For as of this which thou art inne,
Be that thou seist it is a sinne,   *(80)*
And sinne may no pris deserve,
Withoute pris and who shal serve,
I not what profit mihte availe.
Thus folweth it, if thou travaile,
Wher thou no profit hast ne pris,
Thou art toward thyself unwis:
And sett thou mihtest lust atteigne,   *although*
Of every lust thende is a peine,
And every peine is good to fle;
So it is wonder thing to se,   *(90)*
Why such a thing shal be desired.
The more that a stock is fired,   *log*
The rathere into aisshe it torneth;   *sooner*
The fot which in the weye sporneth   *stumbles*
Fulofte his heved hath overthrowe;

Thus Love is blind and can noght knowe
Wher that he goth, til he be falle:
Forthy, bot if it so befalle
With good conseil that he be lad,
Him oghte forto ben adrad.   (100)
For conseil passeth alle thing
To him which thenkth to ben a king;
And every man for his partye
A kingdom hath to justefye,
That is to sein his oghne dom.   judgement
If he misreule that kingdom,
He lest himself, and that is more   loses
Than if he loste ship and ore
And al the worldes good withal:
For what man that in special   (110)
Hath noght himself, he hath noght elles,
Nomor the perles than the shelles;
Al is to him of o value:
Thogh he hadde at his retenue
The wide world riht as he wolde,
Whan he his herte hath noght withholde
Toward himself, al is in vein.
And thus, my sone, I wolde sein,
As I seide er, that thou arise,
Er that thou falle in such a wise   (120)
That thou ne miht thyself rekevere;
For Love, which that blind was evere,
Makth alle his servantz blinde also.
My sone, and if thou have be so,
Yit is it time to withdrawe,
And set thin herte under that lawe,
The which of Reson is governed
And noght of Will. And to be lerned,
Ensamples thou hast many on

Of now and ek of time gon,   (130)
That every lust is bot a while;
And who that wole himself beguile,
He may the rathere be deceived.
My sone, now thou hast conceived
Somwhat of that I wolde mene;
Hierafterward it shal be sene
If that thou lieve upon my lore;   trust
For I can do to thee nomore
Bot teche thee the rihte weye:
Now ches if thou wolt live or deie.   (140)

A: My fader, so as I have herd
Your tale, bot it were ansuerd,
I were mochel forto blame.
My wo to you is bot a game,
That fielen noght of that I fiele;
The fielinge of a mannes hiele   heel
May noght be likned to the herte:
I may noght, thogh I wolde, asterte,
And ye be fre from al the peine
Of love, wherof I me pleigne.   (150)
It is riht esy to comaunde,
The hert which fre goth on the launde   hart; glade
Not of an oxe what him eileth;
It falleth ofte a man merveileth
Of that he seth an other fare,   behave
Bot if he knewe himself the fare,   condition
And felt it as it is in soth,
He sholde don riht as he doth,
Or elles werse in his degre:
For wel I wot, and so do ye,   (160)
That love hath evere yit ben used,
So mot I nedes ben excused.

Bot, fader, if ye wolde thus
Unto Cupide and to Venus
Be frendlich toward myn querele,
So that myn herte were in hele
Of love which is in my briest,
I wot wel thanne a betre prest
Was nevere mad to my behove.   advantage
Bot al the whiles that I hove   (170)
In noncertein betwen the tuo,
And not if I to wel or wo
Shal torne, that is al my drede,
So that I not what is to rede.
Bot for final conclusion
I thenke a supplicacion
With pleine wordes and expresse
Write unto Venus the goddesse,
The which I preye you to bere
And bringe ayein a good ansuere.   back
Tho was betwen my prest and me   (181)
Debat and gret perplexete:
My resoun understod him wel,
And knew it was soth everydel
That he hath seid, bot noght forthy
My will hath nothing set therby.
For techinge of so wis a port
Is unto love of no desport;   consolation
Yit mihte nevere man beholde
Reson, wher love was withholde,   (190)
They be noght of o governance.
And thus we fellen in distance,   disagreement
My prest and I, bot I spak faire,
And thurgh my wordes debonaire
Thanne ate laste we acorden,
So that he seith he wol recorden

To speke and stonde upon my side
To Venus bothe and to Cupide;
And bad me write what I wolde,
And seith me trewly that he sholde   (200)
My lettre bere unto the queene.
And I sat doun upon the grene
Fulfilt of loves fantasye,
And with the teres of my ye
In stede of enke I gan to write
The wordes whiche I wolde endite
Unto Cupide and to Venus,
And in my lettre I seide thus.

   The wofull peine of loves maladye,
Ayein the which may no physique availe,   (210)
Myn herte hath so bewhaped with sotye,   confused; folly
That wher so that I reste or I travaile,
I finde it evere redy to assaile
My resoun, which that can him noght defende:
Thus seche I help, wherof I mihte amende.

Ferst to Nature if that I me compleigne,
Ther finde I hou that every creature
Som time ayer hath love in his demeine,   in the year
So that the litel wrenne in his mesure
Hath yit of kinde a love under his cure;   (220)
And I bot on desire, of which I misse:
And thus, bot I, hath every kinde his blisse.   except

The resoun of my wit it overpasseth,
Of that Nature techeth me the weye
To love, and yit no certein she compasseth
Hou I shal spede, and thus betwen the tweie
I stonde, and not if I shal live or deie.

For thogh Reson ayein my will debate,
I may noght fle, that I ne love algate.

Upon myself is thilke tale come, (230)
Hou whilom Pan, which is the god of Kinde,
With Love wrastlede and was overcome:
For evere I wrastle and evere I am behinde,
That I no strengthe in al myn herte finde,
Wherof that I may stonden eny throwe; pang
So fer my wit with love is overthrowe.

Whom nedeth help, he mot his helpe crave,
Or helpeles he shal his nede spille:
Pleinly thurghsoght my wittes alle I have,
Bot non of hem can helpe after my wille; (240)
And als so wel I mihte sitte stille,
As preye unto my lady eny helpe:
Thus wot I noght wherof myself to helpe.

Unto the grete Jove and if I bidde,
To do me grace of thilke swete tunne,
Which under keye in his celier amidde
Lith couched, that fortune is overrunne,
Bot of the bitter cuppe I have begunne,
I not hou ofte, and thus finde I no game; pleasure
For evere I axe and evere it is the same. (250)

I se the world stonde evere upon eschange,
Nou windes loude, and nou the weder softe;
I may sen ek the grete mone change,
And thing which nou is lowe is eft alofte;
The dredfull werres into pes fulofte
They torne; and evere is Danger in o place,
Which wol noght change his will to do me grace.

Bot upon this the grete clerc Ovide,
Of Love whan he makth his remembrance,
He seith ther is the blinde god Cupide, (260)
The which hath Love under his governance,
And in his hond with many a firy lance
He woundeth ofte, ther he wol noght hele;
And that somdiel is cause of my querele.

Ovide ek seith that love to parforne
Stant in the hond of Venus the goddesse,
Bot whan she takth hir conseil with Satorne,
Ther is no grace, and in that time, I gesse,
Began my love, of which myn hevinesse
Is now and evere shal, bot if I spede: (270)
So wot I noght myself what is to rede.

Forthy to you, Cupide and Venus bothe,
With al myn hertes obeissance I preye,
If ye were ate ferste time wrothe,
Whan I began to love, as I you seye,
Nou stint, and do thilke infortune aweye,
So that Danger, which stant of retenue
With my lady, his place may remuc. remove

O thou Cupide, god of Loves lawe,
That with thy dart brennende hast set afire (280)
Myn herte, do that wounde be withdrawe,
Or yif me salve such as I desire:
For service in thy court withouten hire
To me, which evere yit have kept thin heste,
May nevere be to Loves lawe honeste.

O thou, gentile Venus, Loves queene,
Withoute gult thou dost on me thy wreche; vengeance

159

Thou wost my peine is evere aliche grene
For love, and yit I may it noght areche:
This wold I for my laste word beseche,   (290)
That thou my love aquite as I deserve,
Or elles do me pleinly forto sterve.

   Whanne I this supplicacioun
With good deliberacioun,
In such a wise as ye nou wite,   know
Hadde after myn entente write
Unto Cupide and to Venus,
This prest which hihte Genius
It tok on honde to presente,
On my message and forth he wente   (300)
To Venus, forto wite hire wille.
And I bod in the place stille,
And was there bot a litel while,
Noght full the montance of a mile,
Whan I behield and sodeinly
I sih wher Venus stod me by.
So as I mihte, under a tre
To grounde I fell upon my kne,
And preide hire forto do me grace:
She caste hire chiere upon my face,   (310)
And as it were halvinge a game   half in jest
She axeth me what is my name.
'Ma dame,' I seide, 'John Gower.'
'Now John,' quod she, 'in my pouer
Thou most as of thy love stonde;
For I thy bille have understonde,
In which to Cupide and to me
Somdiel thou hast compleigned thee,
And somdiel to Nature also.
Bot that shal stonde among you tuo,   (320)

For therof have I noght to done;
For Nature is under the mone
Maistresse of every lives kinde,
Bot if so be that she may finde
Som holy man that wol withdrawe
His kindly lust ayein hir lawe;   *natural; desire*
Bot sielde whanne it falleth so,   *seldom*
For fewe men ther ben of tho,
Bot of these othre inowe be,
Whiche of here oghne nicete   *folly*
Ayein Nature and hire office   (331)
Deliten hem in sondry vice,
Wherof that she fulofte hath pleigned,
And ek my court it hath desdeigned
And evere shal; for it receiveth
Non such that kinde so deceiveth.

For al onliche of gentil love   *refined*
My court stant alle courtz above
And takth noght into retenue
Bot thing which is to kinde due,   (340)
For elles it shal be refused.
Wherof I holde thee excused,
For it is manye dayes gon,
That thou amonges hem were on
Which of my court hast ben withholde;
So that the more I am beholde
Of thy desese to commune,   *take account*
And to remue that fortune,
Which manye dayes hath the grieved.   *thee*
Bot if my conseil may be lieved,   (350)
Thou shalt ben esed er thou go
Of thilke unsely jolif wo,   *unhappy*
Wherof thou seist thin herte is fired:
Bot as of that thou hast desired

After the sentence of thy bille,
Thou most therof don at my wille,
And I therof me wole avise.
For be thou hol, it shal suffise:
My medicine is noght to sieke
For thee and for suche olde sieke,   (360)
Noght al per chance as ye it wolden,
Bot so as ye be Reson sholden,
Acordant unto Loves kinde.
For in the plit which I thee finde,
So as my court it hath awarded,
Thou shalt be duely rewarded;
And if thou woldest more crave,
It is no riht that thou it have.'

   Venus, which stant withoute lawe
In noncertein, bot as men drawe   uncertainty
Of rageman upon the chance,   (371)
She leith no peis in the balance,
Bot as hir liketh forto weye;
The trewe man fulofte aweye
She put, which hath hir grace bede,
And set an untrewe in his stede.
Lo, thus blindly the world she diemeth   judges
In Loves cause, as tome siemeth:
I not what othre men wol sein,
Bot I algate am so besein,   treated
And stonde as on amonges alle   (381)
Which am out of hir grace falle:
It nedeth take no witnesse,
For she which seid is the goddesse,
To whether part of love it wende,   whichever
Hath sett me for a final ende
The point wherto that I shal holde.   decision; hold to

162

For whan she hath me wel beholde,
Halvynge of scorn, she seide thus:
'Thou wost wel that I am Venus,   *know*
Which al only my lustes seche;   *(391)*
And wel I wot, thogh thou beseche
My love, lustes ben ther none,
Whiche I may take in thy persone;
For loves lust and lockes hore   *grey*
In chambre acorden neveremore,
And thogh thou feigne a yong corage,
It sheweth wel be the visage
That olde grisel is no fole: *grey nag; foal*
There ben fulmanye yeres stole   *(400)*
With thee and with suche othre mo,
That outward feignen youthe so
And ben withinne of pore assay.   *quality*
Myn herte wolde and I ne may
Is noght beloved nou adayes;
Er thou make eny suche assayes
To love, and faile upon the fet,
Betre is to make a beau retret;   *graceful*
For thogh thou mihtest love atteigne,
Yit were it bot an idel peine,   *(410)*
Whan that thou art noght sufficant
To holde Love his covenant.
Forthy tak hom thin herte ayein,   *recall*
That thou travaile noght in vein,
Wherof my court may be deceived.
I wot and have it wel conceived,
Hou that thy will is good inowh;
Bot mor behoveth to the plowh,
Wherof the lacketh, as I trowe: *thee*
So sitte it wel that thou beknowe   *(420)*
Thy fieble astat, er thou beginne

Thing wher thou miht non ende winne.
What bargain sholde a man assaye,   venture upon
Whan that him lacketh forto paye?
My sone, if thou be wel bethoght,
This toucheth thee; foryet it noght:
The thing is torned into was;
That which was whilom grene gras,
Is welked hey at time now.   withered
Forthy my conseil is that thou   (430)
Remembre wel hou thou art old.'
  Whan Venus hath hir tale told,
And I bethoght was al aboute,
Tho wiste I wel withoute doute,
That ther was no recoverir;
And as a man the blase of fir
With water quencheth, so ferd I;   fared
A cold me cawhte sodeinly,
For sorwe that myn herte made
My dedly face pale and fade   (440)
Becam, and swoune I fell to grounde.
And as I lay the same stounde,   time
Ne fully quik ne fully ded,
Me thoghte I sih tofor myn hed
Cupide with his bowe bent,
And lich unto a parlement,
Which were ordeigned for the nones,   occasion
With him cam al the world at ones
Of gentil folk that whilom were
Lovers, I sih hem alle there   (450)
Forth with Cupide in sondry routes.
Myn yhe and as I caste aboutes,
To knowe among hem who was who.
  I sih wher lusty Youthe tho,
As he which was a capitein,

Tofore alle othre upon the plein
Stod with his route well begon,   adorned
Here hevedes kempt, and therupon   combed
Garlandes noght of o colour,
Some of the lef, some of the flour,   (460)
And some of grete perles were;
The newe guise of Beawme there,   fashion; Bohemia
With sondry thinges wel devised,
I sih, wherof they ben queintised.   adorned
It was al lust that they with ferde,   pleasure; went
Ther was no song that I ne herde,
Which unto love was touchende;
Of Pan and al that was likende
As in pipinge of melodye
Was herd in thilke compaignye   (470)
So lowde, that on every side
It thoghte as al the hevene cride
In such acord and such a soun
Of bombard and of clarion   bass shawm
With cornemuse and shallemele,   bagpie; shawm
That it was half a mannes hele
So glad a noise forto hiere.
And as me thoghte, in this manere
Al freish I sih hem springe and dance,   (479)
And do to Love her entendance   service
After the lust of youthes heste.   command
Ther was inowh of joye and feste,
For evere among they laghe and pleye,
And putten care out of the weye,
That he with hem ne sat ne stod.
And overthis I understod,
So as myn ere it mihte areche,
The moste matiere of her speche
Was al of knihthood and of armes,

And what it is to ligge in armes   (490)
With love, whanne it is achieved.

*   *   *

   Cupido, which may hurte and hele
In Loves cause, as for myn hele
Upon the point which him was preid
Cam with Venus, wher I was leid
Swounende upon the grene gras.
And, as me thoghte, anon ther was
On every side so gret presse,   crowd
That every lif began to presse,
I wot noght wel hou many score,   (500)
Suche as I spak of now tofore,
Lovers, that comen to beholde,
Bot most of hem that weren olde:
They stoden there at thilke tide,
To se what ende shal betide
Upon the cure of my sotye.   folly
Tho mihte I hiere gret partye
Spekende, and ech his oghne avis
Hath told, on that, an other this:
Bot among alle this I herde,   (510)
They weren wo that I so ferde,
And seiden that for no riote   revelry
An old man sholde noght assote;   act foolishly
For as they tolden redely,
Ther is in him no cause why,
Bot if he wolde himself benice;   make a fool of
So were he wel the more nice.   foolish
And thus desputen some of tho,
And some seiden nothing so,

166

Bot that the wilde loves rage   (520)
In mannes lif forberth non age;
Whil ther is oile forto fire,
The lampe is lihtly set afire,
And is fulhard er it be queint,   quenched
Bot only if it be som seint,
Which God preserveth of His grace.
And thus me thoghte, in sondry place
Of hem that walken up and doun
Ther was diverse opinioun:
And for a while so it laste,   (530)
Til that Cupide to the laste,
Forth with his moder full avised,
Hath determined and devised
Unto what point he wol descende.
And al this time I was liggende
Upon the ground tofore his yhen,
And they that my desese sihen
Supposen noght I sholde live;
Bot he, which wolde thanne yive
His grace, so as it may be,   (540)
This blinde god which may noght se,
Hath groped til that he me fond;
And as he pitte forth his hond
Upon my body, wher I lay,
Me thoghte a firy lancegay,   lance
Which whilom thurgh myn herte he caste,
He pulleth oute, and also faste
As this was do, Cupide nam
His weye, I not where he becam,
And so dede al the remenant   (550)
Which unto him was entendant,
Of hem that in avision
I hadde a revelacion,

So as I tolde now tofore.

    Bot Venus wente noght therfore,
Ne Genius, whiche thilke time
Abiden bothe faste byme.
And she which may the hertes binde
In Loves cause and ek unbinde,
Er I out of my trance aros,   (560)
Venus, which hield a boiste clos,   box; hidden
And wolde noght I sholde deie,
Tok out mor cold than eny keye
An oignement, and in such point
She hath my wounded herte enoignt,
My temples and my reins also.   loins
And forth withal she tok me tho
A wonder mirour forto holde,
In whiche she bad me to beholde
And taken hiede of that I sihe;   (570)
Wherinne anon myn hertes yhe
I caste, and sih my colour fade,
Myn yhen dimme and al unglade,
My chiekes thinne, and al my face
With elde I mihte se deface,
So riveled and so wo besein,
That ther was nothing full ne plein,
I sih also myn heres hore.
My will was tho to se nomore
Outwith, for ther was no plesance;   (580)
And thanne into my remembrance
I drowh myn olde dayes passed,
And as Reson it hath compassed,
I made a liknesse of myselve
Unto the sondry monthes twelve,
Wherof the yeer in his astat
Is mad, and stant upon debat,

That lich til other non acordeth.
For who the times wel recordeth,
And thanne at Marche if he beginne, (590)
Whan that the lusty yeer comth inne,
Til Augst be passed and Septembre,
The mihty youthe he may remembre
In which the yeer hath his deduit delight
Of gras, of lef, of flour, of fruit,
Of corn and of the winy grape.
And afterward the time is shape
To frost, to snow, to wind, to rein,
Til eft that Mars be come ayein: afterwards
The winter wol no somer knowe, (600)
The grene lef is overthrowe,
The clothed erthe is thanne bare,
Despuiled is the somerfare, array of summer
That erst was hete is thanne chele.
    And thus thenkende thoghtes fele, many
I was out of my swoune affrayed,
Wherof I sih my wittes strayed,
And gan to clepe hem hom ayein.
And whan Resoun it herde sein
That Loves rage was aweye, (610)
He cam to me the rihte weye,
And hath remued the sotye folly
Of thilke unwise fantasye,
Wherof that I was wont to pleigne,
So that of thilke firy peine
I was mad sobre and hol inowh.
    Venus behield me than and lowh,
And axeth, as it were in game,
What Love was. And I for shame
Ne wiste what I sholde ansuere; (620)
And natheles I gan to swere

169

That be my trouthe I knew him noght;
So ferr it was out of my thoght,
Riht as it hadde nevere be.
'My goode sone,' tho quod she,
'Now at this time I lieve it wel,
So goth the fortune of my whiel;
Forthy my conseil is thou leve.'   let go

    'Ma dame,' I seide, 'be your leve,
Ye witen wel, and so wot I,   (630)
That I am unbehovely   unsuitable
Your court fro this day forth to serve:
And for I may no thonk deserve,
And also for I am refused,
I preye you to ben excused.
And natheles as for the laste,
Whil that my wittes with me laste,
Touchende my confession
I axe an absolucion
Of Genius, er that I go.'   (640)
The prest anon was redy tho,
And seide, 'Sone, as of thy shrifte
Thou hast ful pardoun and foryifte;
Foryet it thou, and so wol I.'

    'Myn holy fader, grant mercy,'
Quod I to him, and to the queene
I fell on knes upon the grene,
And tok my leve forto wende.
Bot she, that wolde make an ende,
As therto which I was most able,   (650)
A peire of bedes blak as sable   rosary
She tok and heng my necke aboute;
Upon the gaudes al withoute
Was write of gold, *Por reposer*.   for your rest
'Lo,' thus she seide, 'John Gower,

Now thou art ate laste cast,
This have I for thin ese cast,
That thou nomore of love sieche.
Bot my will is that thou besieche
And preye hierafter for the pes, (660)
And that thou make a plein reles
To Love, which takth litel hiede
Of olde men upon the nede,
Whan that the lustes ben aweye:
Forthy to thee nis bot o weye,
In which let Reson be thy guide;
For he may sone himself misguide,
That seth noght the peril tofore.
My sone, be wel war therfore,
And kep the sentence of my lore (670)
And tarye thou my court nomore,
Bot go ther vertu moral duelleth,
Wher ben thy bokes, as men telleth,
Whiche of long time thou hast write.
For this I do thee wel to wite, know
If thou thin hele wolt pourchace,
Thou miht noght make suite and chace,
Wher that the game is nought pernable; proper
It were a thing unresonable,
A man to be so overseye. imprudent
Forthy tak hiede of that I seye; (681)
For in the lawe of my comune fellowship
We ne noght shape to comune, communicate
Thyself and I, nevere after this.
Now have I seid al that ther is
Of love as for thy final ende:
Adieu, for I mote fro the wende.'
And with that word al sodeinly,
Enclosid in a sterred sky,

171

Venus which is the qweene of Love,   (690)
Was take in to hire place above,
More wiste I nought wher she becam.
And thus my leve of hire I nam,
And forth with al the same tide
Hire prest, which wolde nought abide,
Or be me lief or be me loth,
Out of my sighte forth he goth,
And I was left with outen helpe.
So wiste I nought wher of to yelpe,
Bot only that I hadde lore   lost
My time, and was sory ther fore.   (701)
And thus bewhapid in my thought,
Whan al was turnid in to nought,
I stod amasid for a while,
And in my self I gan to smile
Thenkende uppon the bedis blake,
And how they weren me betake,
For that I shulde bidde and preye.
And whanne I sigh non othre weye
Bot only that I was refusid,   (710)
Unto the lif which I hadde usid
I thoughte nevere torne ayein:
And in this wise, soth to sein,
Homward a softe pas I wente,
Wher that with al myn hol entente
Uppon the point that I am shrive
I thenke bidde whil I live.   pray

  He which withinne dayes sevene
This large world forth with the hevene
Of His eternal providence   (720)
Hath mad, and thilke intelligence
In mannis soule resonable

172

Hath shape to be perdurable,   *eternal*
Wherof the man of his feture   *fashioning*
Above alle erthly creature
Aftir the soule is immortal,
To thilke Lord in special,
As He which is of alle thinges
The creatour, and of the kinges
Hath the fortunes uppon honde,   (730)
His grace and mercy forto fonde
Uppon my bare knes I preye,
That He this lond in siker weye   *secure*
Wol sette uppon good governance.
For if men takin remembrance
What is to live in unite,
Ther is no staat in his degree
That noughte to desire pes,
With outen which, it is no les,
To seche and loke in to the laste,   (740)
Ther may no worldes joye laste.
    Ferst forto loke the clergye,
Hem oughte wel to justefye
Thing which belongeth to here cure,
As forto praye and to procure
Oure pes toward the hevene above,
And ek to sette reste and love
Among ous on this erthe hiere.
For if they wroughte in this manere
Aftir the reule of charite,   (750)
I hope that men shuldin se
This lond amende.
               And ovir this,
To seche and loke how that it is
Touchende of the chevalerye,   *nobility*
Which forto loke, in som partye

Is worthy forto be comendid,
And in som part to ben amendid,
That of here large retenue
The lond is ful of maintenue, (760)
Which causith that the comune right
In fewe contrees stant upright.
Extorcioun, contekt, ravine
Withholde ben of that covine,
Alday men hierin gret compleignte
Of the desease, of the constreignte,
Wher of the poeple is sore oppressid:
God graunte it mote be redressid.
For of knighthode thordre wolde
That they defende and kepe sholde (770)
The comun right and the fraunchise   priveleges
Of Holy Cherche in alle wise,
So that no wikke man it dere,   harm
And ther fore servith sheld and spere:
Bot for it goth now other weye,
Oure grace goth the more aweye.
   And forto lokin ovirmore,
Wher of the poeple pleigneth sore
Toward the lawis of oure lond,
Men sein that trouthe hath broke his bond (780)
And with brocage is goon aweye,   bribery
So that no man can se the weye
Wher forto finde rightwisnesse.
   And if men sechin sikernesse   certainty
Uppon the lucre of marchandye,   profit; trade
Compassement and tricherye   scheming
Of singuler profit to winne,
Men sein, is cause of mochil sinne,
And namely of divisioun,
Which many a noble worthy toun (790)

Fro welthe and fro prosperite
Hath brought to gret adversite.
So were it good to ben al on,
For mechil grace ther uppon   much
Unto the citees shulde falle,
Which mighte availle to ous alle,
If these astatz amendid were,
So that the vertus stodin there
And that the vices were aweye:
Me thenkth I dorste thanne seye,   (800)
This londis grace shulde arise.
    Bot yit to loke in othre wise,
Ther is a stat, as ye shul hiere,
Above alle othre on erthe hiere,
Which hath the lond in his balance:
To him belongith the leiance   allegiance
Of clerk, of knight, of man of lawe;
Undir his hond al is forth drawe
The marchant and the laborer;
So stant it al in his power   (810)
Or forto spille or forto save.
Bot though that he such power have,
And that his nightes ben so large,
He hath hem nought withouten charge,
To which that every king is swore:
So were it good that he ther fore
First un to rightwisnesse entende,
Wherof that he him self amende
Toward his God and leve vice,
Which is the chief of his office;   (820)
And aftir al the remenant
He shal uppon his covenant
Governe and lede in such a wise,
So that there be no tirandise,
Wherof that he his poeple grieve,

Or ellis may he nought achieve
That longith to his regalye.
For if a king wol justifye
His lond and hem that beth withinne,
First at him self he mot beginne,   (830)
To kepe and reule his owne astat,
That in him self be no debat
Toward his God: for othre wise
Ther may non erthly king suffise
Of his kingdom the folk to lede,
Bot he the King of hevene drede.
For what king sett him uppon pride
And takth his lust on every side
And wil nought go the righte weye,
Though God His grace caste aweye   (840)
No wondir is for ate laste
He shal wel wite it may nought laste,
The pompe which he secheth here.
Bot what king that with humble chere
Aftir the lawe of God eshuieth
The vices, and the vertus suieth,   follows
His grace shal be suffisant
To governe al the remenant
Which longith to his duite;
So that in his prosperite   (850)
The poeple shal nought ben oppressid,
Wherof his name shal be blessid,
For evere and be memorial.
    And now to speke as in final,
Touchende that I undirtok
In englesh forto make a book
Which stant betwene ernest and game,
I have it maad as thilke same
Which axe forto ben excusid,

And that my bok be nought refusid   (860)
Of lered men, whan they it se,
For lak of curiosite:
For thilke scole of eloquence
Belongith nought to my science,
Uppon the forme of rethorique
My wordis forto peinte and pike,   choose
As Tullius som time wrot.
Bot this I knowe and this I wot,
That I have do my trewe peine
With rude wordis and with pleine,   (870)
In al that evere I couthe and mighte,
This bok to write as I behighte,   promised
So as siknesse it soffre wolde;
And also for my dayes olde,
That I am feble and impotent,
I wot nought how the world is went.
So preye I to my lordis alle
Now in myn age, how so befalle,
That I mot stonden in here grace:
For though me lacke to purchace   (880)
Here worthy thonk as by decerte,
Yit the simplesse of my poverte
Desireth forto do plesance
To hem undir whos governance
I hope siker to abide.   securely
    Bot now uppon my laste tide
That I this book have maad and write,
My muse doth me forto wite,
And seith it shal be for my beste
Fro this day forth to take reste,   (890)
That I nomore of Love make,
Which many an herte hath overtake,
And ovirturnid as the blinde

177

Fro Reson in to lawe of Kinde;
Wher as the wisdom goth aweye
And can nought se the rihte weye
How to governe his oghne estate,
Bot everyday stant in debat
Withinne him self, and can nought leve.
And thus forthy my final leve   (900)
I take now for evere more,
Withoute makinge any more,
Of Love and of his dedly hele,
Which no phisicien can hele.
For his nature is so divers,
That it hath evere som travers   disadvantage
Or of to moche or of to lite,
That pleinly may noman delite,
Bot if him faile or that or this.
Bot thilke love which that is   (910)
Withinne a mannes herte affermed,
And stant of charite confermed,
Such love is goodly forto have,
Such love may the body save,
Such love may the soule amende,
The hihe God such love ous sende
Forthwith the remenant of grace;
So that above in thilke place
Wher resteth love and alle pes,
Oure joye may ben endeles.   (920)

BOOK ONE   (Macaulay i. ll. 1-332; 1235-1864)

1-7.   This recalls the concern in the Prologue with division and
discord in church and state. But though 'the world is al miswent'
Gower professes himself unable to put the world to rights. Instead
he will talk of love, a subject of universal interest.

23.   'Can control the degree of love.'

64.   'For it is not long since.'

196.   For a discussion of Genius and his role in the poem, see
Introduction.

245-6.   The detailed review of the Seven Deadly Sins or 'vices' con-
forms to medieval confessional practice.

304-32.   The peril which can ensue from misuse of one's sight reflects
the medieval preoccupation with the eye as a door to the soul.

505ff.   The tale of Florent, similar in several respects to the tale told
by Chaucer's Wife of Bath, has no known source (see Bennett
(1968)pp. 141-2).

510.   *that mochel mihte*: 'who might achieve much.'

596.   'Of natural bodily humours.'

604.   'By astrology or natural signs.'

663.   *goud inowh*: 'abundant wealth.'

865.   *tok thanne chiere on honde*: 'was then cheerful.'

919.   *longe and late*: 'after long delay.'

940.   *fell bot sithe awhile*: 'happened only recently.'

BOOK THREE   (Macaulay iii. ll. 639-780; 1089-1200; 1330-1672)

2ff.   The story of Socrates is told in St Jerome, *Adversus
Jovinianum*, I, 48.   Seneca refers to the story in *De Constantia
Sapientis*, xviii, 5.

100ff.   Gower's source for this tale is Ovid, *Metamorphoses*, Bk III.

212-47.   The strife in the heart of Amans reflects the conflict between
the medieval abstraction *Will* 'self-will, wilfulness, blind impulse' and
Wit, the Middle English gloss on *intellectus* 'the rational faculty'.

256ff.   The tale of Pyramus and Thisbe is based on *Metamorphoses*, IV. Chaucer tells the same tale in *The Legend of Good Women*, ll. 706-923. Mainzer, in *Medium Aevum* XLI (1972), argues for the medieval *Ovide moralise*, written between 1291 and 1328, as an additional source.

462.   *Danger*, a personification of the lady's aloofness, acts as the lady's guardian, and stands between Amans and the attainment of his love.

554.   *upon the bridal chiewe*: 'to champ the bit.'

BOOK FOUR   (Macaulay iv. ll. 1083-1501; 1596-1810;
                                                      2701-3301)

20.   'That under his lord's protection.'

163ff.   There is no known source for the tale of Rosiphilee, but close analogues are found in the twelfth-century *De amore* by Andreas Capellanus and the Breton *Lai du Trot* (see Bennett (1968) pp. 147-8).

407-10. 'That she does not withhold her love, nor delay in turning her youthful inclinations to marriage.'

442-3.   'Through merit love is achieved the sooner in many places.'

444ff.   The references are specifically to religious campaigning. Fighting took place against the heathen Prussians and Tartars, while Rhodes was a crusader stronghold. Chaucer's Knight in *The Canterbury Tales* has also seen service in Prussia and the Mediterranean. There is an interesting similarity in the view regarding the motivation behind crusading between Amans in the *Confessio Amantis* and Blanche in Chaucer's *Book of the Duchess*, ll. 1015-34.

644.   'If he may go to sleep.'

713.   In England between the fourteenth and sixteenth centuries the term 'carol' denoted a poem intended to be sung, often with an accompanying dance. Although many carols took Christmas themes as their subject, other topics, both religious and secular, were not excluded. The distinctive feature was the carol's structure,

composed of uniform stanzas with a refrain sung at the beginning, and repeated after each stanza. See R. L. Greene, *A Selection of English Carols*, Oxford 1962.

729.   The story of Troilus and his love for Criseyde is told in Benoit's *Roman de Troie* (1160), Boccaccio's *Il Filistrato* (c 1338) and, most importantly, in Chaucer's *Troilus and Criseyde*, written between 1380 and 1386 and addressed to 'moral Gower'.

862ff.   The source is *Metamorphoses*, XI. The same tale is told, though in less detail, in Chaucer's *Book of the Duchess*. Mainzer argues for the *Ovide moralise* as an additional source.

897.   'There was no lack of care.'

921.   *Chimerie*: '*Cimmeria*: land of darkness.'

987.   'Stems the outward appearance of dreams.'

1132ff.   In *Amores*, I, 13, ll. 39-40, Ovid appeals to Aurora to hold back the dawn; this is a possible source for the prayer of Cephalus.

1156-9.   In medieval cosmology the planet Saturn was associated with slowness, and the sun came under its influence in mid-December. The sun remaining in Saturn's sphere would ensure, therefore, long nights.

BOOK FIVE   (Macaulay v. ll. 445-728; 5505-6074)

152-66.   The classification of jealousy in love as a type of avarice, an unbalanced possessiveness in respect of one's property, in this case one's wife, is paralleled in the *Roman de la Rose*, ll. 8455-9492, where a jealous lover is compared to an avaricious man.

191ff.   Ovid, in the *Ars Amatoria*, II, tells the story of Venus and Vulcan, but Gower does not follow this source very closely.

332ff.   This tale is told in *Metamorphoses*, VI, but freely adapted by Gower, who omits certain passages and adds others (see Bennett (1968) pp. 162-4, and Mainzer, p. 221). Cf. the treatment of the story in Chaucer's *Legend of Good Women*, ll. 2228-2393.

BOOK SIX   (Macaulay vi. ll. 1261-1292; 1391-1781)

29.   The sin of Gluttony in the medieval confessional tradition

has many branches, but Genius touches on only two, Drunkenness and 'Delicacy'. Within the category of 'Delicacy' Genius includes Luxuriousness, Voluptuousness, Fastidiousness, Self-Indulgence and Self-Gratification. The discussion of Self-Gratification leads on to a description of the use of sorcery, which Genius sees as 'the manipulation of nature for self-gratification' (see Peck (1978) p. 130).

20-1.   As a gloss on types of moral blindness 'as bold as blind Bayard' is a proverbial saying in Middle English. Gower is drawing an analogy between the uncontrolled impulses of love and the behaviour of the horse, commonly called Bayard, whose animal nature leads him, lacking the bridle of reason, into the ditch. Cf. Chaucer's use of the same image in *Troilus and Criseyde*, I, l. 232.

33ff.   The story of Ulysses and Telegonus is told in *Metamorphoses*, XIV, *Roman de Troie*, and Guido delle Colonne's *Historia destructionis Troiae* (1287). Macaulay, III, p. 516, argues for the *Roman de Troie* as Gower's immediate source.

BOOK EIGHT   (Macaulay viii. ll. 2009-2499; 2745-3172)
Although the sin of Lechery is the subject of this book, the main discussion turns on incest as a form of lechery. This is followed by the concluding section of the poem in which Amans says farewell to Love.

47.   'And the longer I love the less I know about it.'

116-7.   'When he has not retained possession of his own heart, all is in vain.'

153.   'Does not know what troubles an ox.'

158-9.   'he would behave exactly as the other man, or even worse in his own case.'

209-92.   The verse-form for the complaint is 'rime royal', a seven-line stanza rhyming ababbcc. It is thought to have been first used in English by Chaucer in his short poems *Complaint unto Pity* and *Complaint to his Lady* (see Bennett (1968) p. 165).

244-50.   This refers back to Book Six, ll. 330-50, where Genius, discussing 'Love-Drunkenness', relates that the classical god,

Juppiter, 'as men sein', has two barrels of love wine in his cellar:
one sweet and one bitter. Cupid, the god of Love, serves men from
these two barrels but, being blind, confuses them. Amans complains
that he has drunk 'of the bitter cuppe', and is, therefore, un-
succesful in his pursuit of love.

304.   *montance of a mile*: 'the amount of time needed to travel
a mile.'

359-60. 'A remedy is not to be sought for from me by you and such
other old lovesick ones.'

371.   *rageman*: Seemingly a game of chance in which compli-
mentary or uncomplimentary verses were drawn, unseen, by players
from a roll, and read out to the company. *OED*, s.v. *Ragman*.

462.   A reference to the Bohemian style of dress, introduced into
England by Anne of Bohemia when she married Richard II in
1382. Bennett (1968) p. 168, suggests that the 'new guise' may
refer specifically to costly hair frets.

474-5.   These are all medieval musical instruments.

581-604.   A similar description of the changing of the seasons and
its connection with the span of a man's life is found in *Sir Gawain
and the Green Knight*, ll. 495-535.

653.   *gaudes*: 'the larger beads of a rosary, set at intervals between
the smaller ones.'

687ff.   This section of the *Confessio* has a different wording in
the first version; Gower addresses himself to Richard 'my worthy
king' and is full of praise for his sovereign. The first version also
contains a command from Venus that Gower 'gret wel Chaucer'
and convey to him her message.

> That he upon his latere age,
> To sette an ende of all his werk,
> As he which is myn owne clerk,
> Do make his testament of love,
> As thou has do thy shrifte above,
> So that my court it may recorde.

Gower's disenchantment with Richard accounts for the removal of any reference to him in the second and third recensions of the poem: the excision of the reference to Chaucer in the two later versions is discussed by Fisher, pp. 119-20.

760.   *maintenue*: 'interference in law suits.'

867.   'Tullius' is Cicero, and the reference is to Cicero's *De Inventione* and the pseudo-Ciceronian *Rhetorica ad Herennium*. Both are treatises on literary style and enjoyed great popularity in the Middle Ages.